# SIMPLEX LOCOMOTIVES AT WORK

## ALAN M. KEEF

**ABOVE:** A pair of 10 ton versions of the same machine as shown on the left; these are at Kyong Dong coal mine, also in South Korea. These were built by Alan Keef Ltd (AK 24 & 25 of 1988) to an enquiry that was in hand at the time of the takeover.

**FACING PAGE:** The number 124U168 written on the headstock dates this picture to late 1975 and these are a batch of four 5½ ton 'U' series locomotives in the erecting shop at Bedford. These were shipped to South Korea but no final destination is known.

Lightmoor Press

© Alan M. Keef
and Lightmoor Press 2019

Designed by Nigel Nicholson

British Library
Cataloguing-in-Publication Data
A catalogue record for this book
is available from the British
Library

**ISBN 9781 911038 55 9**

## LIGHTMOOR PRESS

Unit 144B, Lydney Trading Estate,
Harbour Road, Lydney,
Gloucestershire GL15 4EJ

**www.lightmoor.co.uk**

Lightmoor Press
is an imprint of
Black Dwarf Lightmoor
Publications Ltd

Printed in Poland;
www.lfbookservices.co.uk

Other books by Alan Keef
include:

*A Tale of Many Railways:
An Autobiography & History
of Alan Keef Ltd*
Lightmoor Press (2008)
ISBN 978-1-899889-30-3

*Motor Rail Ltd*
Lightmoor Press (2016)
ISBN 978-1-911038-09-2

*Motor Rail Catalogues*
Lightmoor Press (2017)
ISBN 978-1-911038-27-6

Double track is a rarity on narrow gauge industrial railways but there was a short stretch of about a quarter of a mile on the Leighton Buzzard Light Railway just beyond the terminus of the present preserved railway. LBLR No. 2, MR 1383 of 1918, is working a full load of sand towards Billington Road on the outskirts of the town. This is an ex-War Department loco of the open type and the date is 1956. (See page 15.) *Courtesy Frank Jux*

# Photographs and Acknowledgements

I owe an enormous debt of gratitude to all those who have allowed me to use their photographs for this book; without them it would have been nothing. It is invidious to mention names but I feel I must particularly thank John Browning of Queensland, Australia, not only for his generosity with his own collection of photographs but also in pointing me to others who have provided pictures from their collections. I have credited all of them, I hope, correctly and as they would wish. Readers please note that quite a number are copyrighted. There are a few for which I know who the photographer is but I have been completely unable to make contact to request permission to use their picture. They have been credited and I trust you will forgive me. As always with this type of book, thanks must go to Bob Darvill of the Industrial Railway Society for his encyclopaedic knowledge of places and locomotives. Photographs with no accreditation are largely from the collections of Alan and Patrick Keef and the Motor Rail records. My thanks are also due to Patrick for providing technical corrections to the manuscript. Finally, as to whether I have my facts right in every caption may be another matter entirely, but any mistakes are assuredly mine and I look forward to the corrections that will surely come!

I have organised the book effectively by continent although inescapably there is greater content for the UK and Ireland than places further afield. It is perhaps surprising how much has been available from Australia and the Far East but I regret the paucity from India. The problem seems to be that on the sub-continent steam outlived small diesel locos and the former was what the photographers went to see.

This fairly well known photograph carries an almost illegible caption that these are the first five 20hp tractors built at the 'New Works', to be known as Simplex Works from then on. The lead locomotive is WDLR (War Department Light Railways) LR 2366, recorded as MR 1645; the quintet were despatched on 30th April 1918. The person from whom this photograph came many years ago said that the lady on the left (then aged 16) would become his mother, and standing next to her is John Dixon Abbot. This scene is more commonly published without all the works and office staff.
*Courtesy John Reyner*

# Introduction

This book could be considered as a spin-off from my two previous volumes, on the history of Motor Rail Ltd and a review of the catalogues and sales literature that it produced over the years. The intention here is to portray the company's locomotives at work in the many and varied places that they worked around the globe. Motor Rail Ltd really was an international company whose locomotives could be found in countries from Argentina to Zambia and most places in between. In this day of e-mails and the internet it is astonishing to consider how this was achieved seventy to eighty years ago.

In many ways it is the internet that has made this book possible as photographs of Simplex locomotives are posted on various sites such as Flickr and thus it is possible to find images that have not been seen at least too often before. Much of Motor Rail's production, certainly in later years, was sold through Railway Mine & Plantation Equipment Ltd (RMP) and it has to be regretted that their extensive photographic library was destroyed when that company was taken over by German interests.

Initially a very brief history of the company is required followed by a synopsis of the principle types of locomotive that the company made over the years. Their locomotives were very standardised and close to being mass produced. Peter Cross, who worked for the company all his life and probably knew more about it than anyone before or since, used to recall that the works would produce four locomotives and a dumper, week in, week out, and more when required.

ABOVE: The above is taken from a slide, presumably used for a talk, and shows in graphic form the concentration of sales around the world probably in the early 1970s.

BELOW: Remarkably, there is in Cheltenham a drain cover bearing the name of Phoenix Foundry of Lewes. This carries the lettering ESE standing for East Sussex Engineering, which Phoenix Foundry became in 1971.

Surprisingly, the company's origins do not lie in the world of light railways at all even if it is in that field that it made its name. The founder, John Dixon Abbott, was initially involved with East India Tramways Ltd, which company operated the 4ft gauge street tramway system in Karachi, India – now Pakistan. This started off as a steam tramway operation, reverted to horses and then under Abbott's leadership converted to petrol driven tramcars in 1910; remarkably early in the history of internal combustion traction. That the operation continued until 1975 and was never electrified is testimony to the success of the initial designs. For this purpose he designed and patented the Dixon Abbott gearbox, which gave equal speeds in either direction of travel, and this was not just highly successful but was the key to most of the locomotives and other vehicles that were subsequently built.

To pursue the potential of this development and the manufacture of tramcars for Karachi and elsewhere, the Motor Rail & Tram Car Co. Ltd was set up in March 1911. This company continued to be the effective owner of East India Tramways and supplied most of its requirements until it was sold to local interests at the time of the partition of India in 1949. Initially the Motor Rail & Tram Car Co. did not have any manufacturing facilities of its own and the first tramcars were contracted out to be built by the Phoenix Ironworks in Lewes, Sussex. The engines and gearboxes were at this time bought in as complete units having been made by David Brown Ltd. In 1916 the company moved to Bedford where it continued to act as a design office but still sub-contracted actual manufacture to the Bedford Engineering Co. It was not until early 1918 that it acquired what became the Simplex Works in Elstow Road, Bedford, and thereafter manufactured its products in its own premises.

Having seen in his travels how the Germans were stockpiling light railway equipment and locomotives, John Abbott offered the British military a locomotive based around his gearbox but was rebuffed. However, by 1916 the Western Front had fought itself to a standstill and interest in light railways re-emerged. After completing an initial order for just three locomotives (called tractors at the time) the company went on to produce no fewer than 724 of its 20hp tractors and 334 of the 40hp design. At one stage this involved producing no less than twenty-five locomotives per week! Abbott had always foreseen that his locomotives would be ideal for the construction and quarrying industries. Thus when hostilities ceased he was able to buy back a large number that he then remanufactured to be sold on into those industries, and indeed anywhere else where there was material to be moved. The company continued to manufacture tramcars for Karachi, mostly in chassis-only form with bodies to be built locally. As will be seen, it did the same for a number of other operations and had high hopes of the potential market. In this it was probably well ahead of its time and these hopes were never fully realised. A pair of quite sophisticated cars built in 1927 for the Onda–Castelon line in Spain was the last in this line of work. In the light of this the company changed its name to Motor Rail Ltd in 1931 and it is by this name that it will be known throughout this book.

In the interwar years it developed its design for locomotives in both standard and narrow gauge form and built machines up to 120hp and 20 tons in weight. Some of these locomotives put in sixty years of industrial service before being scrapped or sold into preservation – no mean achievement by any standards. During the Second World War a large number of locomotives were sold to the War Office but it was nowhere near the bonanza of the Great War. Indeed many were still in their packing cases at war's end. Over the years the company

**ABOVE:** A fully armoured 40hp tractor 'somewhere in France' during the First World War. War Department Light Railways (WDLR) locomotive No. 2184 is MR463 of 1918 and had a peripatetic career after the war, finally ending up in In Aberdeen by 1929.

*Courtesy J.A. Peden, IRS collection*

**BELOW:** Works photograph of the motor coach supplied to the Onda–Castelllon Raiway in Spain. Motor Rail excelled themseleves in these vehicle with full internal electric lighting, drop light windows, reversible seating, shaft drive to the bogie and outside coupling rods.

built up an enviable reputation overseas with, for example, some 880 locomotives being sold to South Africa, primarily for the then booming mining industry.

There came to be a long and acrimonious dispute between the company and its South African agent, E.C. Lenning Ltd, which eventually excluded Motor Rail from that market. However, while it lasted the numbers were staggering, such as an order for 200 locomotive in one batch! By comparison, around 550 were sold to the East African countries, primarily for the sisal industry, with roughly the same quantity being divided between India and the Far East.

In 1951 Motor Rail Ltd became a public company; it was itself taken over in 1965, ironically by a subsidiary of Lenning, although the name was retained. This company was in turn sold again in 1972, with a subsidiary company, Simplex Mechanical Handling Ltd, being set up to carry on the original business. This became an independent entity in 1976, with the locomotive side of the business being sold to Alan Keef Ltd in 1987 when the lease of its premises in Bedford ran out and it was deemed not worth moving the business elsewhere.

Motor Rail had a renaissance in the period up to about 1975, when around 200 hydraulic drive locomotives were sold to many countries but largely to Canada, gaining a Queen's Award for Export Achievement along the way, and large numbers of the traditional design continued to be despatched around the globe. Motor Rail had developed a very successful dumper in 1938 and this continued in production until the mid-1960s when a conscious decision was made to cease developing what had become a very successful unit. Following this the company diversified into various other manufacturing fields such as trailers and particularly fork lift truck attachments, with the latter becoming the mainstay of operations. An early diversification was the provision of a hire service for the company's locomotives and, in due course, dumpers. Petrol Loco Hirers, later Diesel Loco Hires (DLH), was initially the brainchild of John Abbott himself, but he was later bought out by Motor Rail and integrated into the main operation. Part of its *raison d'être* was to offer a means

Except for the last few built, the dumpers used modified engine and gearbox from the 20/28 locomotive. MR 8389 of 1947 is believed to be one of only two in preservation.
*Courtesy Moseley Railway Trust*

This 3ft 6ins guage locomotive built by Alan Keef Ltd in 1990 as their AK 37 resurrected the 9 ton design and may still be being used for shunting in Port Harcourt Docks, Nigeria.

by which Simplex locomotives could be tried out by potential customers before actual purchase. It also offered a buffer against slack trading conditions when locomotives were built for the hire company and sold on later.

The company carried on building locomotives as and when orders were obtained, despite the fact that the then parent company was doing its best to abandon that type of work. The final two were built on sub-contract by Alan Keef Ltd prior to the takeover. A small number have been built since, so at least John Abbott's original design lives on.

## LOCOMOTIVE NUMBERING

The system of recording the works numbers of locomotives developed by the Industrial Locomotive Society is used where appropriate. Thus locomotives built by both Motor Rail & Tram Car Co. Ltd and Motor Rail Ltd are designated MR followed by the number and year of build (MR 463 of 1918 or MR 9932 of 1972). When the company changed its name to Simplex Mechanical Handling Ltd the nomenclature became SMH (SMH 103G058 of 1975) and when, in turn, Alan Keef Ltd took over it became AK (AK 50 of 2000). When a locomotive has been rebuilt with major changes to its original form or appearance it carries an R number (AK78R of 2007). So far as this book is concerned the abbreviations for other manufacturers are of no concern.

## MEASUREMENTS

All measurements are in imperial measure except where the build records use the metric system and this will ordinarily only apply to rail gauge. Except where otherwise stated, rail gauge can be assumed to be 600mm/24ins. However, lengths of overseas railways are often quoted in kilometres (km) and this is used where appropriate. Weights are again imperial measure, although Motor Rail did use the American ton of 2,000lbs for locomotives sold into the American sphere of influence. Locomotives were classified as, say, 3½ tons depending on the ballast weights fitted, but in practice this could vary considerably either way depending on such things as engine type, whether cab fitted and any extras such as air brakes or exhaust conditioner. This can be particularly confusing with the 32/42 model.

This is the locomotive with which Motor Rail made its name. Known at the time as a 20hp tractor, 724 were supplied to the military for service worldwide. It was fitted with a Dorman 2JO petrol engine, the Dixon Abbott two-speed gearbox and weighed in at 2½ tons. Taken from a 1948 catalogue, this seems to have been the first time that Motor Rail publicised their achievements during the First World War.

# Locomotive Types

For readers who are not conversant with the products of Motor Rail Ltd there follows a thumbnail sketch of the various types of locomotive they produced. This is unashamedly not comprehensive but covers all the main types of which there are pictures in this book. The illustrations are largely taken from the various leaflets that the company produced over the years although some, especially in later years, are lacking in clarity.

Big brother to the 20hp tractor was this one that weighed 6 tons and was powered by the 40hp 4JO Dorman engine. This is taken from a 1923 catalogue and shows the open version. There was an enclosed type with doors giving protection from rifle fire and an armoured version (see page 5) that could cope with something more serious. A total of 324 of these were supplied to the Western Front and elsewhere.

No doubt for economy of construction the 20hp locomotive built for industrial service after the First World War had straight frames but is otherwise identical to its wartime cousin even to including the Klaxon horn. It was usually sold weighted to 4 tons but the ballast weights could be dispensed with if required. The multi-slot bufferhead has appeared but does not include the Simplex logo that became such a distinctive feature.

Following the First World War, large numbers of these 40hp standard gauge shunters were produced utilising the engine and gearbox arrangement of the 40hp tractor. The last of the type was not built until 1948 and some survived in commercial service until the early 1980s.

The 20/28 was arguably Motor Rail's all-time best seller, being in production from about 1935 to 1959. Except for a few early ones, it was usually fitted with the Dorman 2DWD diesel engine driving a two-speed gearbox, was available in weights from 2½ to 4½ tons and was often cab-fitted and included an exhaust conditioner if to be used underground. This is the machine of which 200 were ordered in one batch for South Africa.

This is the 32/42 which sold almost as well as the 20/28 but seems to have been much less photographed. Fitted with the Dorman 2DL engine and usually a three speed gearbox it was available in weights of 4 to 7 tons. Such things as cab, air brakes and exhaust quenchers were available. This image dates from a 1937 leaflet. The quoted weights for these locomotives is difficult to follow particularly for the 6 and 7 ton range so quite apart from the question of add-ons the figures should be treated with care.

LEFT: Known simply as the 9 ton, this locomotive was built from about 1949 and fitted with the Dorman 3DL engine of 65hp (later the 4LB) and proved popular for surface working overseas. Only one unit ever worked in the UK. There was also a 10 ton version with the 5LB engine of 100hp.

The 12hp 1¼ ton loco was an attempt to produce a small locomotive for a perceived market that may not have existed. It was very much built down to a price (e.g. no springs) and as such was not wholly successful. It was normally fitted the Lister SL2 or SR2 air-cooled engine However, it was the forerunner to the 'G' series.

The 'G' series was a tidy little locomotive of which some 85 were sold notably to the Ghana State Goldmining Corporation and to the Far East. They were fitted with a variety of engines but mostly the Petter PJ2R of 20hp and were usually supplied at 2¼ tons weight. The exception to all the rules was one at standard gauge for Wolverton carriage works where it is still at work.

**ABOVE**: The 40S was the successor to the 20/28 and was built up the time of closure, and beyond by Alan Keef Ltd. Built in weights up to occasionally 5½ tons it was fitted with Dorman 'L' series engines with horsepower increasing from 30 to 48hp over the years. Latterly it was fitted with the Deutz F3L912 air-cooled engine of 40hhp. With this engine it tended to be overpowered and was most successful at 3½ tons and above when also the cab was not quite so cramped.

Likewise, the 60S took over from the 32/42 and was available in weights up to 7 tons. Again the Dorman 'L' series engine was fitted with power increasing from 50 to 72hp and using a beefed up version of the 32/42 three speed gearbox. The 40S and 60S were often bracketed together for advertising and leaflet purposes and again could be fitted with cabs and exhaust quenchers.

Even in the 1960s there was still a call for a light weight standard gauge shunter and this machine at 8 tons filled the bill. It was basically the 60S chassis with an extended wheelbase together with larger and heavier bodywork hung round it. The engine and gearbox remained the same but the driver stood to drive. The last was built in 1974 for use in Guyana.

The largest of the range was this shunter that was available in weights up to 20 tons but was mostly in the 12-14 ton range. It was powered by the Dorman 4DL engine of 85hp although at least one had the 5LB giving 100hp. They were mostly used in the likes of gas works in the UK but a few went overseas.

Due to the poor quality of in-house produced leaflets in later years this is a works photograph of a lightweight 'U' series probably for either Cameroon or Somalia. This one has hydrokinetic, or torque convertor drive, although roughly half those built had hydrostatic transmission. It would have had ballast weights added to the headstocks to bring it up to the more common 8 or 10 tons weight. Designed for mining the cab was optional for surface working. A six-wheel version of this locomotive was designed but never built.

The 'T' series was designed as a larger version of the 'U' series and intended for mining work although in the event was never used as such. Like the 40S and 60S the 'U' and 'T' series tended to be marketed together and in many ways were very similar in concept. Both were usually fitted with Dorman 6DA and later Deutz F6L912 engines of around 100hp, and the 'T' series could be weighted to 14 tons. Both could also be hydrostatic or hydrokinetic drive.

Correctly, these two pictures should be within the Europe section of this book but as it was in the First World War that Motor Rail made its name as a locomotive builder instinct suggests that they should be included here. This well-known photograph of a pair of 20hp tractors hung on the wall of Motor Rail's offices for many years and continues to do the same for Alan Keef Ltd. It shows 'the first train over Vimy Ridge' in April 1917. These are Canadian troops and they had a well-deserved reputation for their use of light railways. From the shape of the brake column support, the lead locomotive is an early one and would have been manufactured by Bedford Engineering Co. In the early days these locomotives carried running numbers that matched the works numbers. Curiously, however, this locomotive has the number 98 whereas the works list does not start until 200!

## British Isles

Neither man nor machine are working very hard in this photograph and the state of the buildings and surrounding trees suggest that this is well back from the front line. However, LR 3009 is MR 1288 and was not despatched until July 1918 so may not have reached France until near to the end of hostilities. This could have been taken during the clearing up operations that carried on for some considerable time after the Armistice. Looking new and smart this is the protected version of the 40hp tractor fitted with the Dorman 4JO petrol engine and would have weighed some 6 tons although no actual figure is recorded.
*Courtesy Industrial Railway Society*

Like a number of pictures herein, this is a posed photograph taken as part of a series for a marketing brochure by the Hendre Ddu Slate Quarry, situated in a remote valley in mid-Wales. The date is 1925 and the locomotive is MR 2059 of 1921. Note the multi-slot coupling block and the side buffers to work on the dumb buffered wagons. The location is Aberangell station on the Dinas Mawddy branch from the Cambrian Railway and the transfer point to the main line. Laid down in the late 1860s, this was effectively a private railway and together with its many branches totalled some seven miles in length serving not only slate quarries but farms, a brick works, sawmills and forestry. One, at least, of the quarries specialised in slate slabs, as seen behind the two gentlemen on the left, which at that time were often used for making the panels of electrical switchgear.

This substantial railway with its embankment, fencing and even telegraph poles was is at Belford Hall in Northumberland and was part of an extensive forestry line. The train load of logs seem to be somewhat precariously balanced on a rake of small wagons and do not appear to be roped down in any way. The locomotive is MR 1074 and was despatched to the Ministry of Munitions on the day after the Armistice in 1918. It almost certainly never reached France as it is recorded that spare parts were supplied to this location in 1920.
*MR&TCo. catalogue,
courtesy Jon Bryant*

In today's world a volunteer operated narrow gauge railway may be an exciting undertaking. However, in the past the reality of commercial operations in mid-winter was not for the faint hearted. This is Leighton Buzzard Light Railway shortly after it had ceased to be an independent organisation in 1958 and the locomotives had been transferred to the sand companies. Arnold's No. 42 has just crossed Swing Swang bridge on its way to Billington Road. The normal load for these locomotives was twenty-four wagons but in this case the train may be a couple of wagons light to allow for the bogie wagon of dried and bagged sand. The drivers used to complain that these ex-WDLR wagons always 'ran heavy'. MR 7933 of 1939 is a 5 ton 32/42 and was originally built for Sir Alfred MacAlpine Ltd's gravel pits at Gresford, near Wrexham; at some stage it was sold to Derbyshire Stone and, via the dealer George Bungey, came to Leighton Buzzard in 1956 as a replacement for an original WDLR 40hp locomotive as seen on page 2.

Over the years the sand quarries around Leighton Buzzard, Bedfordshire, operated in the order of a hundred Motor Rail locomotives, divided between the two principle sand companies Joseph Arnold & Sons Ltd and George Garside Ltd. These were mostly the ubiquitous 20/28 in its 2½ ton form, with a few 3½ ton locos for good measure, and a handful of the 32/42 6 ton model used for the main line to Billington Road Sidings. Here we have one of Garside's fleet leaving the Double Arches quarry complex and crossing Eastern Way with a full train of twelve wagons of sand circa 1959. The absence of a flagman to warn road traffic is surprising but he may be out of shot. The Leighton Buzzard Light Railway started just behind the last wagon of the train where the tracks divided for Garsides to the right and Arnolds straight on. This is MR 7195 of 1937 that was originally supplied, along with twelve others, to Glasgow Corporation Housing Department for their Robroyston housing contract.

In the late 1950s the ironstone mines near Thistleton in south Lincolnshire were the subject of a major development and reconstruction. For this purpose the contractors Balfour Beatty & Co Ltd used a fleet of three 20/28 2ft gauge locomotives, two of which are seen here. Just which is which is not definitive but the nearest locomotive is likely to be MR 21615, new to Balfour Beatty in 1957 for use on their contract at Berkeley Nuclear Power Station, Gloucestershire. The one behind is MR 9000 of 1956; this is actually a rebuild of MR 8642 of 1942, when it was supplied to the War Office, and subsequently rebuilt with a new works number for Sir Robert McAlpine Ltd. Note the big black boxes next to the radiator which are exhaust conditioners for underground working.
*Courtesy S.A. Leleux*

This operation of Thomas E. Gray Ltd at Isebrook, near Kettering, Northamptonshire, was unusual even by 1978. The 2ft gauge line brought ganister, a type of sand used for refractory purposes, which was tipped into standard gauge wagons that were part of what was by then an internal system, with the main line connection having been taken out some thirty years previously. MR 5881 of 1935 seems to have been initially hired by Diesel Loco Hirers to the Ham River Grit Co. at Harlington, Middlesex, who then bought it a few months later. In 1965 it came to Joseph Arnold & Sons Ltd who used it until 1969, when it moved to Isebrook with the system here being closed in 1982. It replaced a similar loco built three years later than this one!
*Courtesy Kevin Lane*

The 32/42 was probably Motor Rail's second-best-selling locomotive after the 20/28 but photographs of it tend to be rare. As a consequence this slightly cropped picture is included. The locomotive is unidentified but is almost certainly one of a batch of four built to the unusual gauge of 2ft 11ins for London Brick Co. Ltd for use at their Newton Longville Works, near Bletchley, Buckinghamshire. The heavy cast iron ballast weights, both under and over the headstocks, that bring the weight up to 7 tons can clearly be seen. Electric light is also fitted but the loco may not have had its own charging system. This is the transfer point to the aerial ropeway to the works and the train is loaded with empties to be returned to the pit. The date is 1961 and all four locomotives were scrapped four years later when no doubt the system was replaced by conveyor belts or the pit was worked out. *Courtesy S.A. Leleux*

In this Motor Rail photograph, another of the quartet rattles off towards the pit where excavator jibs can be seen in the distance. The inbound loaded track can be seen to the left and judging by the number of jacks in evidence some track repairs are in progress.

Very definitely a Simplex at work! In a cloud of diesel exhaust this one brings a wagon-load of potatoes out of a siding at Wasps Nest Farm, presumably to make up a train with wagon No. 12 on the right and maybe to then transfer the empty wagon behind it into the siding for loading. This is the railway at Nocton, Lincolnshire, which was by this time owned by and supplied potatoes to Smiths Crisps Ltd in Lincoln. There were at one time some 130 miles of railways at fifty different locations serving the potato farms of the Fenland but this was by far the largest with twenty-odd miles of track and six locomotives to operate the trains. Most of the equipment and particularly the wagons came as First World War surplus, although the first three locomotives were supplied new in 1920 to the wartime 20hp 'tractor' design. These were dieselised in 1934 (with cabs being added at the same time) and this picture dates from a private visit to the system on a normal working day in 1955. The vehicle on the extreme left looks very like the corner of a tank wagon, several of which were used to carry water to the remote homesteads in this flat Fenland area.    © R.P. Lee, NGRS collection

Earls Barton Silica Co. Ltd was typical of the small operations all over the country for which the light railway came into its own. Here we have MR 8731, originally built for the Ministry of Supply in 1941 and despatched to Market Drayton, Shropshire. It was then with Westbury Brick & Pipe Co., also in Shropshire, for an unspecified period before being sold by Motor Rail to Earls Barton as a secondhand locomotive in 1963. In 1965 the photographer recorded the loco as 'rope shunting', suggesting that it is moving up towards the train so that a rope can be attached to the last wagon to move the whole assemblage forward, when it can then get to the back of the train to push it into the tipping shed. For the record, Alan Keef Ltd cleared all the remaining track from this site in 1972 and brought in a Hudson Hunslet locomotive for the purpose.    Courtesy S.A. Leleux

Simplex locomotives were something of a rarity in the north Wales slate quarries where Ruston & Hornsby tended to be the preferred manufacturer. However, Maenofferen Quarries in Blaenau Ffestiniog had had a 4 ton locomotive, purchased in 1920, so that they should buy another in 1961 seems entirely reasonable. MR 20073 was originally supplied to the City of Birmingham Water Dept and despatched to New Works, Knighton, Radnorshire in 1950 (see page 42). The records state that it was returned to Motor Rail before being sold to Maenofferen in 1961. It is seen here in 1963, shunting a train of rubbish wagons out onto one of the waste tips that are such a feature of the Blaenau Ffestiniog landscape. Although the track is fine just here, these wagons were fitted with double flanged wheels (there is one lying beside the locomotive) for places where it was not quite so good. *Courtesy S.A. Leleux*

Possibly one of the earliest private preservation projects was this 2ft gauge line belonging to Brian Goodchild, running through woodland near Leamington Spa. The locomotive is MR 8575 of 1940, one of the many built for the War Office at that time. The records state that at some stage it was returned to Motor Rail, was with a Mr Burleigh of Wembley in 1947 and with the dealer, George Bungey, in 1955. Somewhere along that journey it acquired the cab seen here. Together with all the equipment from this site it passed through Alan Keef Ltd's hands in 1970 and moved back into commercial use with Mixconcrete Aggregates Ltd of Northampton. Lurking in the background can just be seen a Hudson Hunslet 20hp locomotive that would also have been built for the War Office.
*Collection Dan Quine*

At Goldenvale Ironworks, near Tunstall, Stoke on Trent. In September 1970, MR 8602 of 1940 is looking a bit lost amongst the pile of scrap metal, a part of which it may ultimately have become. Note the circular crane magnet at rest beside the wagon. This would be used to load the tipping skip with the contents then being unloaded onto the conveyor on the right. The overall canopy on the loco is probably more to protect the driver from falling debris than the weather. One half of the bonnet is raised so perhaps he is either about to start or stop the engine.

The Motor Rail records are unusually forthcoming about this locomotive. It was built for the Buckland Sand & Silica Co. Ltd of Reigate, Surrey. In 1945 it was with Herts Plant Hire Ltd of St Albans and in 1949 a replacement engine was quoted to Savages Ltd of Kings Lynn. This works was closed around six months later and the site cleared for housing. *Courtesy S.A. Leleux*

Dating back to 1921 is MR 2036 which appears to be still active at the Ashwood Dale quarry of Derbyshire Stone Ltd in 1964. It has had a new and more enclosed cab built onto it, somewhat similar to the original, but giving better protection from the Peak District weather. It is highly likely that the original Dorman 4JO petrol engine would have been replaced by a diesel at this date. The original order is in the name of J.W. Horton, the Derbyshire County Surveyor, with a later annotation that it was with Derbyshire Stone but, unfortunately, no date given. This locomotive and its compatriot dating from 1936 were both scrapped in 1971, but fifty years service has to have proved the success of original design. *© RCTS Archive*

This British Railways shunter is MR 1931, an 8 ton 40hp shunter which was despatched on Christmas Eve 1919 to the Lowestoft permanent way depot of the Great Eastern Railway, there replacing the horses previously used. History repeated itself when in 1925 it was transferred to Brentwood Goods Yard where for some years it had the name 'Peggy' chalked on its side, after the horse that had formerly done the shunting! It was variously renumbered by the L&NER and British Railways to finally become Class 'Y11' No. 15098. It remained here until withdrawn and scrapped in 1956. Judging by the shiny wheels and rails it was in very regular use in 1954.
*Courtesy Brian Pask*

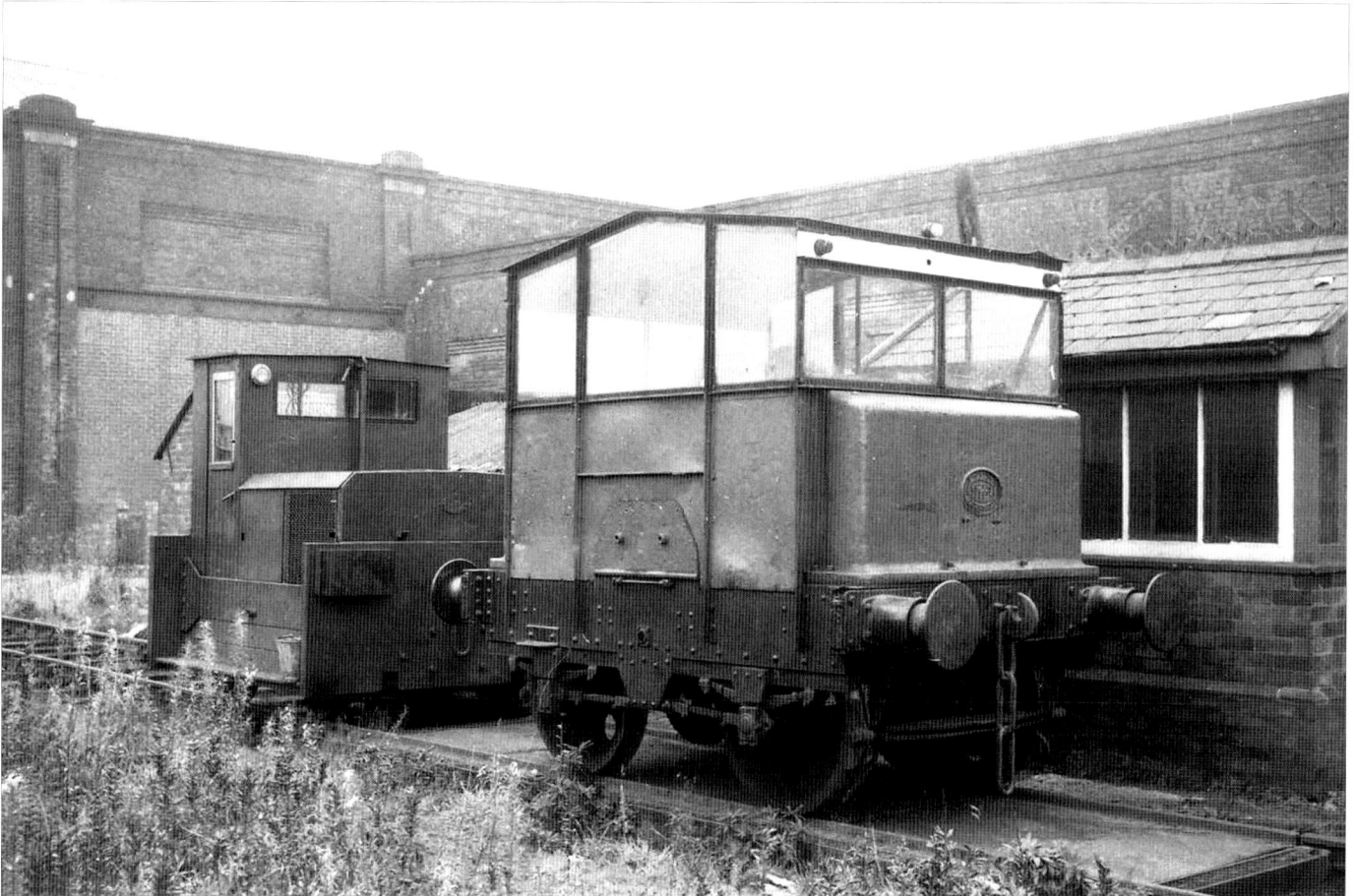

MR 9009 of 1949 was the last of what might be termed the 'old style' Simplex standard gauge locomotive. It was supplied to Tweedale Smalley (1920) Ltd for their Globe Works at Castleton, near Rochdale. The company was taken over by F.W. Woolworth Ltd in 1964, who in turn took delivery of MR 9930, possibly in the same year although no delivery date or destination is recorded. Both weighed 8 tons and were fitted with Dorman 4DWD and 3LB engines of 45/63hp and 60hp respectively. At that time the premises were a major distribution depot for Woolworth's. The earlier loco is now in preservation with the East Lancashire Railway at Bury.
*Courtesy S.A. Leleux*

Of later years this was the largest of the standard gauge locomotives that Motor Rail produced. MR 5757 of 1955 weighs 12 tons and they could be supplied a couple of tons heavier. This one was fitted with the Dorman 4DL engine of 65/85hp and, judging by the air tank visible next to radiator, was fitted with air brakes. Models built some years later were fitted with an overall bonnet which improved their appearance and made them more look like a 'real' locomotive. Note here the protective plates fitted front and rear in case those RSJs should decide to slide in a sudden stop. The site is the distribution depot of Redpath Dorman Long at East Greenwich in south London and the date is 1971.

MR 9921 was built for stock in 1958, transferred to Diesel Loco Hirers Ltd in 1959 and sold to the local firm of C.A.E.C. Howard Ltd a year later, who in turn used it at Hemel Hempstead Concrete Co. Ltd in Hertfordshire. Slightly lighter than usual, it is recorded as being 7 tons weight but is still fitted with the Dorman 3LB engine of 50hp. Its purpose in life is amply demonstrated by this photograph. Hemel Hempstead Concrete made lightweight building blocks under the trade name of Hemelite and no doubt considerable quantities of fuel were needed for 'cooking' them in large ovens. It looks as though it is still in ex-works yellow whereas later shots show it painted bright orange.

*Both courtesy S.A. Leleux*

MR9932 of 1972 is an 8 ton shunter and is seen bringing rail containers to the Fort Dunlop storage facility of the Dunlop Rubber Company at Erdington in Birmingham. This is with a Motor Rail driver immediately following delivery. These locomotives were a modified form of the narrow gauge 60S locomotive; in the centre picture, taken at the Bedford works, it can be seen how this was managed. They were arranged for the driver to stand up to drive, the frames were cut away to take the extended axles for standard gauge and the wheelbase extended to the maximum the frame would allow. Finally, the heavy buffer beams and higher cab were 'hung around' the modified chassis. The Dorman 3LD engine and 3-speed gearbox were unchanged. Many years later this locomotive was converted to 24ins gauge and worked for Rare Stone Ltd in Wiltshire. This operation had an interesting career: the stone mine was originally opened for the building of Salisbury Cathedral in 1220; during the Second World War and afterwards it was within a military storage facility, during which time it was re-opened to repair the spire; it finally became a general stone mine upon closure of the military base. In the third picture, MR 9932 can be seen with two large blocks of stone being moved from mine to cutting shed on what had once been the army's roadside tramway. The frame cutaways make a convenient step for the driver!

*Bottom picture courtesy John Stevenson*

This could also be a posed photograph because of two empty trains apparently going in the same direction; or maybe one of them is not actually in use. The place is the Kings Dyke brickworks of Flettons Ltd, near Peterborough, and the date 1970. This may well be a sales/publicity shot in view of what happened next – see below. The right-hand locomotive is MR 8875 of 1944, one of the many built for the War Office at that time. Reputedly most of the locomotives here were bought from a dealer in the early 1960s and were still in their original packing cases! One has to marvel at the number of wagon-loads of clay that would have been needed to excavate the pit in the background.

*© RCTS Archive*

This is the same locomotive at Woodwalton Fen, again not far from Peterborough. Reading between the lines, it would seem that almost the entire railway from Kings Dyke brickworks was sold to this site, including three locomotives. The purpose was a railway some 1½ miles long to move dredged material to form a protective bank against the Great Raveley Drain. This predates the sale of the remaining seven locos to Alan Keef Ltd in 1971, from whence they were distributed far and wide.

*© Gordon Edgar*

The housing in the background indicates just how close to Southend-on-Sea the Cherry Orchard works of Butterley Building Products Ltd was. This picture also shows how a shallow layer of clay was removed from the fields for brick making in much the same way that sand was taken by Pilkingtons at St Helens for making glass (see page 29). The locomotive is a standard 20/28 that has been modified with a quite sophisticated cab and particularly with a change to a Deutz air-cooled engine. This would make it compatible with new locomotives bought in the late 1980s. Note how the original fuel tank has been placed where the radiator would have been. MR 8691 was originally built for the Admiralty and despatched to RN Armament Sub Depot, Camerton, near Cockermouth, Cumberland in January 1942. Here it is nearly fifty years later in 1991.

*Courtesy Toon Steenmeyer*

The clay pit railway at Redland Bricks' Nutbourne Works carried on in use for longer than most because two different types of clay were dug from the same face (the different colours can be seen in the background) and then mixed for various types of brick. In 1986 MR 8678 of 1941 propels a loaded train up towards the tipping dock whilst AK 14 of 1984 returns to the pit with a rake of empties. Not visible here is the fact that the loco has had its original engine replaced with a Lister unit that sticks out of the side by about 6ins! This locomotive had a varied history, starting off in the Diesel Loco Hirers fleet before being sold to the Ightham Brick & Tile Co. Ltd in 1946, with Alf Hardy (perhaps a dealer) in 1946 and the Sussex & Dorking Brick Co. by 1956; it eventually ended up with William Blyth at Far Ings Tileries, Barton-on-Humber, Lincolnshire and indeed still exists (see back cover).

**RIGHT:** Alne Brick Co. Ltd operated a slightly more conventional railway system at their works near York and until quite late in the day too. Here is MR 8694 of 1943 seen in 1988. This locomotive was built for the River Ouse (Yorks) Catchment Board and at some stage was sold, possibly via the dealer George Bungey, to Alne Brick Co. The all-enclosing cab includes the engine, possibly to keep the driver warm. The fuel tank has been moved, which is usually a sure sign that the power unit has been replaced with an air-cooled engine of some sort.

LEFT: Cattybrook Brickworks, Almonsbuury, on the outskirts of Bristol operated a line in their clay pit at the unusual gauge of 2ft 10½ins. The track was made up from mainline bull head rail in GWR chairs and included stub points where required. The two locomotives are MR 5342 and 9215 of 1931 and 1946 respectively. Both were originally built at 3ft gauge for Dinmor Quarries in Anglesey. Some sources quote Cattybrook as 3ft gauge so maybe it depended on where the gauge was measured! The wagons were reputed to be at least fifty years old. The railway closed in 1975 when the pair passed through Alan Keef Ltd's hands and, converted to 2ft gauge, went to Boothby Peat Co. Ltd near Carlisle (see page 31), where they were no doubt scrapped after serving another turn of duty.
*Courtesy Neil Parkhouse collection*

MR 40SD530 of 1987 was in build with Alan Keef Ltd when that company took over the locomotive business of Simplex Mechanical Handling Ltd. It was made for Butterley Building Products Ltd for use at their Star Lane Brickworks, near Southend-on-Sea, and is here seen two years later loading clay in the pit. Unfortunately this railway was closed for a period for the installation of a gas main and was not reopened afterwards despite the protestations of the local management. The locomotive, however, is still in commercial use having been re-gauged to 2ft 8½ins gauge for maintenance use on Volks Electric Railway at Brighton. For this purpose it was also raised very slightly in order to clear the electric pick-up rail and the cab removed to give easier access. The lower picture shows this loco propelling an empty train back to the pit whilst AK 26 of 1988 passes with a loaded train for the works. Noticeable is a reversion to the 20/28 frame which allowed for a more commodious cab although the ballast weights and sanding gear remain the same. This one was actually built for the Cherry Orchard works along with a second one a year later.

*Upper picture courtesy Adrian Nicholls, lower Toon Steenmeyer*

**ABOVE:** Photographs of the railways used by Pilkingtons Glass in the area around St Helens in Lancashire are rare. The photographer took this shot whilst on a field trip from his university in 1969 and the train is somewhat incidental to his purpose. However, it shows how the layer of white silica sand was removed from the fields for the purpose of glass making and the land returned to agriculture at lower right. Pilkingtons bought eleven of these 5 ton 60S Motor Rail locomotives between 1960 and 1969, all built to the unusual gauge of 24⅛ins. The loco looks smart so it may be one of the later ones. Spare a thought for the skill of the dragline driver who, with his bucket swinging on the end of a wire, would require no more than two scoops to fill a wagon. *Courtesy Cliff Bancroft*

In 1979 ex-Pilkingtons loco MR 60S362 of 1968 was converted to 3ft gauge by Alan Keef Ltd for Caledonian Peat Products Ltd. Here seen at their Gardrum Moss, Carnwath, Lanarkshire, it has been considerably modified over time. The raised cab and side walkway became a regular feature of locomotives working peat bogs so that the driver could see over his train. It has been re-engined with an industrial engine of the same Dorman 3LB type but with a radiator attached to the engine, and this can be seen as the black line to the left of the engine compartment. Thus the Simplex radiator has gone allowing space for tools and materials. The hand lever sticking out of the cab suggests a modification of the brakes to allow operation from the platform. It also seems to have been had a hard life as the top half of the cast iron buffer block is broken off.

**RIGHT:** The peat industry was the last major user of traditional industrial light railways in the UK, but all have now closed and moved to countries where environmental concerns are not so great. Extracting peat has been described as quarrying in a plate of porridge and this was where the light railway scored because the weight was spread through rails and sleepers over a large area. This is Bolton Fell, near Brampton, Cumbria, and the aspect is bleak even on a sunny day. This was originally the Boothby Peat Co. Ltd but eventually became William Sinclair Ltd, as is the site below. The works and packing sheds are behind the trees in the distance and MR 7188 of 1937 has a train of empties proceeding to the loading point. The moss is being worked on the milled peat principle where a few inches of peat is skimmed off the surface and stockpiled for transport. In earlier years it was mechanically cut into blocks that were allowed to dry and temporary tracks were laid along the rows to remove the sod peat.

Most of the peat companies rarely bought new locomotives but gathered up secondhand ones and rebuilt them with new engines to suit their particular needs. This one started life with the Ham River Grit Co. Ltd at a gravel pit near Reading.

LEFT: In similar vein, the first loaded train of the day at Auchencorth Moss, not too far from Edinburgh, is with AK 28 of 1989 that was built for Butterley Building Products Ltd for a brickworks near Southend-on-Sea. On the right is MR 21505 of 1955, originally with a sewage works of Reading Corporation, but here on track maintenance duties. Note the apparently excessive amount of sleepering to the track.

*Both © Gordon Edgar*

On a cold and frosty morning in 1989 at Kirkbride, Cumbria, Fisons' No. 3 *Wedholme* makes ready for the day's work. The driver has scraped the frost off the cab windows and may even have his engine running. MR 8885 of 1944 is an ex War Department loco and was probably in the works at the same time as *Digger* below. The loco behind is another of the breed but unidentified and is one of the half dozen or so others on this site.

**ABOVE**: The day has improved and *Wedholme* is making good speed with a trainload of peat. This picture makes it obvious as to why the cab has been raised. Note the headlights for night-time running and the radiator replaced with a tank but in the same place.

**RIGHT**: In 1992 *Kate* (see page 46) on the right is on hire to contractors Taylor Woodrow working in the Woodhead Tunnel (between Manchester and Sheffield), now in use as a cable tunnel by National Grid. To the left is *Digger*, MR 8882 of 1944, an ex-War Department locomotive that was one of the leftovers at Kings Dyke Brickworks (see page 24) and is being used for track maintenance work within the tunnel by Alan Keef Ltd.

At the more remote locations that were not connected to their own works the destination of loaded trains was simply a tipping dock from where the peat was transferred by road to somewhere that it could be packed. This is another William Sinclair operation, at Whim Moss, near Leadburn, Scotland in 1992, where MR 8738 of 1942 looks as though it has unloaded its train and is waiting to return to the moss. This locomotive was originally built for Sir Robert McAlpine Ltd, the contractors, and passed through Motor Rail's hands again in 1949, being then sold to London Brick Co. It is only just recognisable as a 20/28, having been re-engined, fitted with new cab and bonnets, and had added the side platforms common to the industry. The yellow bucket may well be a supply of sand for the second man to drop onto the rails in case of need.

Micklam Fireclay mine, near Lowca, Cumbria, was actually owned by the Workington Iron & Steel Co. Ltd (later part of British Steel Corporation); it provided clay for a brickworks adjoining Lowca colliery, which in turn supplied coal to the steelworks. It is 1971 and once the crew have settled the affairs of the world, MR 9709 of 1952 looks set to depart with a train of small tubs of coal for the steelworks. Both fireclay and coal were extracted from this mine. This 20/28 locomotive of 2ft 6ins gauge was purchased by the Beckermet Mining Co. Ltd who operated in the same area and may well have been part of a conglomerate of small concerns attached to the steelworks.
*Both © Gordon Edgar*

**ABOVE:** 3½ ton MR 6867 of 1934 ambles along with a short train in idyllic surroundings at Marlow Sand & Gravel in Buckinghamshire in 1980. The record states that it was built for a stone quarry in Derbyshire and it looks to be in remarkably original condition except for the radiator which is of the later flat topped 40S design. The train would have been loaded by dragline and hopper identical to that shown below except that Marlow was a wet pit.

*Courtesy Geoff Cryer*

This was a short-lived line at Charlecote in Warwickshire, installed very late in the day for this type of railway in order to reduce noise and dust to adjoining houses. The 22RB dragline fills the hopper and the wagons are loaded under the control of the man in the check shirt. The locomotive has been re-engined with a Deutz engine, which will have reduced its weight (and haulage ability).

In 1979 Simplex Mechanical Handling built three 2ft 6ins gauge 'T' series locomotives for the National Coal Board for a surface line some two miles long at Ledston Luck Colliery in Yorkshire. This transferred coal to Peckfield Colliery for grading and transfer to the main line. With Willison couplers and the 'stack' of ballast weights plainly visible, these weighed 14 tons and were the heaviest locomotives built of later years. Fitted with the Dorman 6DA air-cooled engine rated at 112hp and twin-disc transmission, the company was justifiably proud of them. In the main picture above and on the front cover SMH 101T018 is seen in 1980.

*Courtesy Geoff Cryer*

**ABOVE:** This was a relatively short lived operation and by 1989 all three had passed into Alan Keef Ltd's hands where two were re-gauged to 900mm to spend some years shunting wagons through the repair shop on the Channel Tunnel contract.

**RIGHT:** In 1999 101T018 suffered a further reincarnation for the Leighton Buzzard Railway. The locomotive was effectively reversed, had extended headstocks and footplate fitted to allow for an independently mounted and soundproofed cab with dual controls. It retained the original engine and transmission arrangements and the weight was reduced to 12 tons. As such it became AK 59R and is seen here working hard as it pulls a heavy passenger train away from Pages Park station in May 2018. By the time this book goes to press *Beaudesert* will have worked as many years at Leighton Buzzard as it did in industrial service. *Courtesy Mervyn Leah*

Motor Rail did not supply many locomotives to the National Coal Board and those that they did were entirely for surface working. If truth be told they were simply not up to the brutal usage meted out to the Hunslet and Hudswell Clarke locomotives used underground. However, here we have SMH 60SD755 of 1980 working at Wheldale Colliery, near Castleford, Yorkshire, in 1982. Of 2ft 6ins rail gauge it was fitted with a Deutz F4L912 air-cooled engine of 62hp and was built to the restricted weight of 6 tons necessary with this engine. The bodywork was changed with these locomotives to enclose the space formerly occupied by the radiator. It has the dubious honour of being the penultimate locomotive to be built at Bedford.
*Courtesy John Phillips*

**ABOVE:** MR 40S280 of 1966 and built at 4½ tons is on stockyard duties at New Stubbin Colliery in 1978. It has had a new cab made for it that extends over the rear ballast weight, necessitating a modified coupling but doubtless giving improved access for the driver. The string of little tubs which form its train are from another era but maybe the shaft cage or trackage underground will not accept anything larger.

**RIGHT:** This locomotive was later converted to 3ft gauge by the NCB at New Silverwood Colliery. Following the wholesale closure of collieries it found its way to the Isle of Man where it is used for maintenance work on either the steam railway or the Manx Electric as required. *Both courtesy A.J. Booth per Industrial Railway Society*

Simplex Mechanical Handling built two 3ft gauge 'T' series locomotives for use by Blue circle Cement at their gypsum quarry at Kilvington in Nottinghamshire. These were 101T007 of 1974 and 101T016 of 1976, and here we see the former pushing a loaded train towards the tipping dock where the gypsum was transferred to the main line (at right) for distribution to the company's works around the country. To the left can be seen the newer of the pair, when still very new, heading out with an empty train. Note the bullhead rails and chairs used in the loop line, possibly reclaimed from main line sidings. SMH had this picture mounted for exhibition use.

Both locomotives moved into preservation with the Lord O'Neil at Shanes Castle, near Antrim, in Northern Ireland, for use on his tourist railway within the castle grounds. When that line closed the pair were split up with the more modern going to the Bush Mills & Giants Causeway Railway. Around 1990 101T016 has a train comprised of a rake of four-wheel street tramcars from Belgium. Just visible on this murky day are a set of air horns on the cab roof from a Canadian National Railways locomotive. When used these could be heard the other end of Lough Neagh some 25 miles away!

In glorious surroundings alongside Lough Finn, 101T007 has been rebuilt along the lines of *Beaudesert* at Leighton Buzzard and is now AK 78R of 2007. It retains its Deutz F6L912 air-cooled engine of 104hp. This is a trial run following delivery and it is working push/pull with restored railcar No. 18 from the County Donegal Railways. The Fintown Railway operates along a short stretch the former Glenties branch of CDR and the original station building can be seen in the far distance.

Of later years, Severn Trent Water Authority was Motor Rail's principle UK customer for new locomotives. These were for use in sludge treatment works, principally at Minworth on the outskirts of Birmingham. These two pictures from the records suggest that, despite the connotations, it was not such an unpleasant place after all. The water was filtered through the sand beds in the open ponds that can be seen and the railway used for the removal of waste and its replacement with clean sand. These shots are from a series of photographs used for publicity purposes and are of a batch of three locomotives, SMH 40SD501/2/3, supplied in 1975.

In common with the 60S, these Deutz engine locomotives had extended bonnets covering where the radiator used to be. Upon arrival at Minworth the first job was to cut half of these away to provide space for the second man to stand! Also added were additional grab rails and pockets for the wooden poles used for re-railing wagons.

Severn Trent Water were one of the few organisations in the UK to use 'G' series locomotives. They had two, SMH 104G060 and 063 of 1976, at their Newstead works near Stoke-on-Trent. Photographs of these were also used by the company for publicity, so this shot of one of them on somewhat uneven track would have been taken shortly after delivery. At the time there was a worldwide shortage of small diesel engines and these were fitted with Kirloskar RA2 engines, an Indian version of a Deutz engine – a choice that was never repeated! 104G063 had the unusual distinction of moving from Newstead into preservation and then back into industry in the stock yard of a private coal mine in Northumberland, before finally becoming a preserved locomotive.

Neither Motor Rail, nor subsequently Simplex Mechanical Handling, were renowned for building anything out of the ordinary, but every now and again they excelled themselves. Here we have a 'G' series, 103GA078 of 1978, built to standard gauge for shunting vehicles in Wolverton Carriage Works. Fitted with a Petter PJ2 engine of 20hp, it unsurprisingly weighed in at 3 tons which was well over the norm of 2¼ tons for these locos. It is very shiny and new in this MR picture, with design engineer John Palmer driving, but, so far as is known, is to this day still doing the job it was built for.

MR 7059 of 1938 was ordered by a Mr Alex Myles of Chester for the Eaton Hall Railway but by 1950 was working on the 15ins gauge Romney, Hythe & Dymchurch Railway in Kent. Whilst basically a 20/28 it is unusual in that the frame has to be noticeably wider to cater for the very narrow gauge. Re-engined and fitted with hydraulic transmission, it is still in use on maintenance trains.
*Courtesy Toon Steenmeyer*

Altogether more spectacular was Motor Rail's one foray into the leisure market. MR 22224 of 1966, named *Cheyenne*, was built for Wicksteed Park at Kettering and was delivered with a fanfare of 'Wild West' characters with whom various publicity shots were taken. The basic 40S locomotive is very obvious in the axleboxes, bonnet and cab line, but has been suitably embellished to give it the American appearance. The carriages were also supplied with the locomotive but whether Motor Rail built them themselves is not recorded. This railway is relatively unknown but carries in excess of 250,000 passengers on its two mile circuit every season, which, by any standards, is an awful lot of people.

Perhaps a less well known picture of a well-known locomotive. *Mary Ann*, on the Ffestiniog Railway, incorrectly carries the works number 507 of 1917 but is one of the 40hp tractor type built in profusion for World War One. Neither the exact location of this picture nor the occasion seem to be recorded, but it is said to include the great and the good of the preservation society at that time. The date is variously stated as being 1954 to 1956 and it could be the first through trip to Blaenau Ffestiniog in the new era, or a precursor to it. The only certainty is that it is the redoubtable Allan Garraway standing on the footplate. The locomotive was acquired by the Welsh Highland Railway when both railways were part of the Col. Stephens 'empire' for off-season services.      *Courtesy Dan Quine*

By 1990 *Mary Ann* had been fitted with what became known as it's 'pagoda' body and vacuum brakes enabling her to shunt passenger rolling stock. Actually working a passenger train is unusual but perhaps this is a short-working special or deputising for a failed steam locomotive, Either way, here she is on a Down train at Minffordd station looking very smart in what looks like new paint.
*Courtesy Roger Marks*

Is this the ultimate garden railway? At a private location in Oxfordshire is a re-enactment of the Darjeeling Himalaya Railway. MR 21619 of 1957 was originally built as a 2½ ton locomotive of 2ft 6ins gauge fitted with the standard 2DWD engine for the Midland Moss Litter Co. Ltd at their Fannyside Moss at Longrigend in the lowlands of Scotland. For this operation it has been re-gauged to 2ft, the weight increased to 3½ tons, fitted with a Perkins 3.152 engine and air brakes to act as yard shunter on this quite steeply graded line. Here it is bringing a replica DHR Third Class carriage out of what is really the locomotive shed for transfer to the carriage shed on the right. Note the water tower at left for steam locomotives. The replica DHR station is behind these buildings.

The picture at left is not quite what it seems however, being a railway in a garden as opposed to a garden railway. It utilised prefabricated Jubilee track laid on planks across a smart garden in Cheltenham so that a large swimming pool could be constructed in that garden. An excavator was moved in once across sheets of plywood and everything, but everything, else went in or out by rail. Thus the garden was completely undisturbed. The locomotive is MR 21513 of 1955, originally supplied to Frankley Pumping Station in Birmingham (see next page). It has been re-engined with a Dorman 2LB engine and thus has non-original bonnets and exhaust. Two skips are being brought back from the public road where their loads will have been tipped for disposal elsewhere. The date is circa 1984.

Over a period of twelve years from 1892, Birmingham Corporation built a series of reservoirs in the Elan Valley near Rhayader in mid Wales to supply the growing City of Birmingham with clean water. Along with this they built a pipeline for 73 miles to bring water all the way from Wales by gravity. In 1952 an additional reservoir of comparable size was built to increase the supply; this in turn required the pipeline to be enlarged and in the late 1950s a parallel pipeline 6ft in diameter was laid. For this a series of light railways were used and moved forward as the work progressed. These railways varied but were generally about a mile in length. Here the additional pipe has been installed in its own bridge over the GWR Stourbridge Junction to Kidderminster line near Hagley station and the temporary railway is using it for its own purposes. The locomotive is the standard 2½ ton 20/28 and other pictures suggest that two wagons was the maximum load, possibly due to gradients. Note that in the days before hi-viz waterproof clothing the driver is using the radiator to dry out his various coats; also the mound of surplus soil behind the wagons. *Courtesy John Tennent*

MR 21513 of 1955 was featured on the previous page working in sophisticated garden surroundings. Here it is in its more normal environment with Taylor Woodrow Ltd carrying out repairs to the Woodhead cable tunnel near Sheffield in 1990. It was originally supplied for the contract featured above and Frankley Pumping Station was the storage point from which equipment was then distributed as required. This loco moved around considerably following completion of that job, having been at various times with Llanberis Lake Railway, Redland Bricks and Knebworth Park before being exported to Angola through RMP in 1991. The manrider was a carriage built for an amusement park that almost instantly went bankrupt and has come down in the world for this operation.

Photographs of the prototype 12hp locomotive, MR 26001 of 1963, on trial with Bedford Silica Sand Mines Ltd, a small sand quarry in the Leighton Buzzard area, are reasonably well known (see page 10), but this one taken from the opposite direction is less so, even if the driver is the same. There was an apparent need at the time for a locomotive smaller than the 40S to compete with the well-known Lister machine and this was an attempt to build one 'down to a price', which was then under £1,000. It weighed in at only 1¼ tons and was powered by a Lister SL2 air-cooled engine of 12hp. Its Achilles heel was that it was unsprung and used what were effectively wagon wheelsets supplied by Allens of Tipton. They were sold largely through RMP to some of Motor Rail's regular customers but until the design metamorphosed into the 'G' series were generally unsuccessful. The prototype eventually went to a salt works in Greece.

Only a couple were sold into service in the UK and at centre left is MR 26016 of 1966 in 'undressed' state with Cumberland Moss Litter Industries Ltd, at Kirkbride, near Carlisle. This was always a somewhat ramshackle organisation but the loco appears to be posed with a 'new' peat wagon. The warning gong (left over from East India Tramways perhaps!) is very prominent.
© A.J. Booth
per Industrial Railway Society.

Just a glimpse of MR 26014 in 2007 delivering new timber for a playground on the Perrygrove Railway in the Forest of Dean, Gloucestershire. It was originally built to 2ft 6ins gauge for Richardsons Moss Litter Co. Ltd for use on their Gretna moss near Carlisle and has been re-gauged to 15ins for Perrygrove. Named *Workhorse*, it is just that on this popular tourist railway.
Courtesy Michael Crofts

The Royal Naval Armaments Depot at Milford Haven in west Wales was unusual, for this country, in having its railway system in metre gauge – but then the Navy also had others of the same gauge at Ernesettle, near Plymouth and inside the Rock of Gibraltar. A 3½ ton 40S, MR 22144, was supplied in 1962 but the record does not give a delivery address. The 'power bulge' in the bonnet cover is also unusual but that may be because the engine has been flameproofed. Aside from instructing drivers that all loads must be sheeted and roped before moving off, the writing on the cab side states that it has been electrilly (*sic*) tested on 24/7/80. In this picture from 1982, note the outside wheels because of the rail gauge.
© *J.M. Hutchings*

Both these photographs are taken in summertime but demonstrate how the weather can change when high in the Pennines close to Shap summit on the West Coast Main Line. This is Shap Granite Co. Ltd and both locomotives have an interesting history. The first, seen in July 1957, was built as MR 1895 for Samuel Gee & Sons of Ripley in 1919 as a 4 ton petrol loco. It was repurchased via William Jones Ltd and McAlpine in late 1923, then 'reconstructed' as MR 3694 before being sold to Shap Granite in 1924. It was dieselised in 1933. The lower picture, in August 1971, is MR 7463 of 1939. Originally a DLII hire loco it is recorded as being converted to 3½ tons for delivery 'a.s.a.p.' to Cumberland. The cab style is to allow clearance through a restricted tunnel under a road. The track looks immaculate and that would have led to a very efficient railway, but then ballast was probably not a problem.
*Courtesy B. Roberts*
*per Industrial Railway Society*
*and © Gordon Edgar*

British Industrial Sand Ltd, formerly Joseph Boam Ltd, operated an extensive 1ft 11½ins system within their sand pits at Middleton Towers, near Kings Lynn, Norfolk. They were great users of Motor Rail locomotives, with a fleet of 32/42's that was superseded by five 50hp/60S machines. This is the last of the line, 7 ton MR60S318 of 1966, on a wet and miserable day in 1970. The train is conveying spoil from a foundry sand screen to a tip. Note the very large silencer mounted across the front ballast weight in an effort to reduce the noise levels for the driver, an aspect of all MR locomotives that would not be tolerated today.

This was the third Motor Rail standard gauge locomotive at Middleton Towers, with them being upgraded from an 8 ton 40hp machine of 1919 through a 10 ton version in 1933 to MR 5754 of 1948, being 65/85hp and 15 tons weight. The unusual front bonnet cover is unique to Middleton Towers and is to prevent too much sand dropping into 'the works' when the loco is passing underneath the wagon loading shutes. The date is 1970 but, alas, the engine broke a crankshaft in 1975 and was scrapped shortly afterwards. The narrow gauge system soldiered on until closure in 1977.
*Both © Roy Burt per Gordon Edgar*

MR 7215 of 1938 was built for the Ham River Grit Co. Ltd of Sussex, although it spent the bulk of its working life with Arnold's at Leighton Buzzard, probably through the dealer George Bungey of Heston. By whatever means, it wound up derelict with the Vale of Teifi Railway in west Wales. It was bought from there by Alan Keef Ltd in 1991 and fitted with a new Deutz F3L912 engine together with new cab and bodywork. Named *Kate*, it was hired to a succession of contractors before being sold to George Metcalf Ltd for use at Chat Moss, near Manchester. Here it is with Taylor Woodrow Ltd at their Southall segment plant in 1995. It was also on the Rochdale canal site described below.

MR 21282 of 1960 was a stock locomotive built for Diesel Loco Hirers and subsequently sold on to Eastwoods Flettons for use in one of their brickworks. It subsequently went to Fison's peat operation at Kirkbride, near Carlisle, before moving on in derelict condition to Alan Keef Ltd. The original engine was replaced with a Deutz F3L912 air-cooled engine with some additional weight added before history repeated itself and it embarked on a peripatetic career of being on hire to various contractors around the country. In this photograph it is with Dew & Co. Ltd for the dredging of the Rochdale canal in 1992. The track was laid along the towpath so that the sludge could be moved in these somewhat precariously arranged lorry skips for removal from site. The locomotive lives on, now being in preservation at the Lea Bailey goldmine site near Ross-on-Wye.

© *Gordon Edgar*

This picture epitomises the spectacular nature of the 2ft 6ins gauge railway that was installed by Sir Archibald Birkmyre to carry guests and their guns from Dalmunzie House onto his grouse moor. Two and a half miles long, it included a zig-zag with gradients of at least 1:20 and a substantial viaduct across a ravine. This is *Glenlochsie*, MR 2086 of 1922, with the closed coach that had four swivelling chairs, drop lights in the ends and curtains at the sides. There was also a 'Second Class' carriage with tramcar type reversible seats for four and little weather protection. This equipment joined *Dalmunzie*, MR 2014 of 1920, which together with two flat wagons was used to build the line. The line itself closed in 1978 and the equipment was sold, only to be repurchased with some new rail also being acquired for a possible reincarnation that never happened. The locomotives and rolling stock were all built by Motor Rail but despite *Glenlochsie* being lost in a runaway in the 1960s, the remainder still exists, albeit in a tragic state of disrepair.

Dalmunzie was not the only grouse moor railway in Scotland although it was probably the better known; there was also another belonging to Lord Lithgow on Duchal Moor to the south-west of Glasgow. This was a much more extensive line than Dalmunzie with possibly as much of seven miles of track that included two triangular junctions and delivered the guns direct to the butts. Added to that, it was moved about over the years as requirements changed. For this Motor Rail supped two 20hp locomotives in 1922, MR 2171 and 2097, but the rolling stock was supplied by their near neighbours in Bedford, J. & F. Howard Ltd. These two are seen crossing Blacketty Water on a very rare enthusiast visit in 1970. Curiously, 2171 is recorded as being a 4 ton machine whereas 2097 is under 2 tons. Perhaps experience gained between the deliveries dictated that four tons was too heavy. The railway had a renaissance in the 1980s when a third locomotive was added to the fleet, MR 8700 of 1941. This was a standard 20/28 and had been built for Sir Alfred McAlpine Ltd but came to Scotland from Joseph Arnold & Sons Ltd at Leighton Buzzard. Following the theft of upwards of a mile of track (how on earth did the thieves remove it from such a remote location?), the line closed completely and the equipment remains in store. *Courtesy Hamish Stevenson, per Mark Greenwood*

With the general demise of the light railway as a means of internal transport in favour of lorries, dumpers or conveyor belts, many locomotives were taken over for use by the growing band of railway enthusiasts and leisure railways. This one was the brainchild of the gravel pit operators, A.J. Mackaness Ltd, who converted their gravel pit near Northampton into the leisure complex of Billing Aquadrome. This is likely to be MR 7031 of 1936, built new as a petrol loco for Mackaness and delivered to Little Billing, but no doubt dieselised by the time of this photograph in 1954. Old skip frames provided bogies for the lengthy rake of articulated carriages that completed the ensemble. I remember riding this railway about 1960 and reporting a broken rail, of which nobody took much notice!
*Courtesy Frank Jux*

The Simplex locomotive with its cross engine and the radiator 'stuck out the front', whilst eminently practical, did not look like everyone's idea of a locomotive, be it steam or diesel. As a consequence, many attempts were made to improve the appearance and make it look like what the public perceived to be a steam locomotive. This is one of the better efforts, with suggestions of a GWR pannier tank engine. It is MR 9978 of 1954, originally built for the Great Ouse River Board, and the conversion was carried out by Track Supplies & Services Ltd of Wolverton who were the franchisees of the railway at the Cotswold Wildlife Park at Burford, Oxfordshire. By the time this shot was taken in 1982 the original 2DWD engine had become decidedly smoky, which was at least appropriate to its new guise.

Also early days for the leisure railway. This 2½ ton 40S is unashamedly in industrial condition circa 1983 with the only concession to passenger working being the provision of an air compressor and prominent air tank in order to provide the continuous braking system to the train that by then had become mandatory. The place is Knebworth House, a short distance north of London. MR 40S273 of 1966 was built for Newalls Insulation & Chemicals Ltd of Washington, Co Durham. The cab is non-original but whether this was added in its industrial days or at Knebworth is not known.

The 'Steamplex' is the result of a conversation in a pub! MR 5877 of 1937 was built for Geenham Plant Ltd and spent its working life on various civil engineering contracts. Having been acquired by enthusiasts in 2013 it was converted to steam power by Alan Keef Ltd, becoming their AK 93R. The single cylinder engine of unknown make or age drives through the original Motor Rail gearbox and chain drive to the wheels thus providing a reverse gear which the engine does not have. The boiler came from a steam boat and the whole setup is remarkably successful. It is based at the Groudle Glen Railway in the Isle of Man and is seen waiting to depart Sea Lion Rocks station with a well loaded passenger train shortly after delivery.

*Courtesy Trevor Nall*

Happy days! The Iron Horse Railroad was the forerunner of the present Leighton Buzzard Railway and persuaded Joseph Arnold & Co. Ltd, who were by then the only company operating over the Leighton Buzzard Light Railway, to allow them to run trains at weekends provided the line was available for sand trains by Monday morning. This is their first public passenger train, for rail fans only, on 3rd March 1968. Bogie wagons had been borrowed from Arnold's for the occasion and those intrepid enough to make the journey had to stand for the whole eight mile round trip. Complete with cycle outriders, the train makes its way alongside Vandyke Road. Note the man with cine camera lying on the roof of the Dormobile van. Having passed the present terminus of the LBR the train is approaching journey's end and close to the point shown on page 15. The passengers still have the return trip to endure! The locomotive is MR 5618 of 1932, supplied to Tarmac Ltd. The IHR obtained it from St Albans Sand & Gravel Ltd for the princely sum of £10, where it had been buried under a heap of sand.                                              *Both courtesy Peter Arnold*

Motor Rail Madness. Nearly fifty years later, in May 2016, a cavalcade of Simplex locomotives was assembled to celebrate 100 years of the start of production of these locomotives in nearby Bedford. This was a record for the number of locomotives from one manufacturer assembled to haul a passenger train. There are sixteen locomotives in this picture, starting with an original War Department 20hp tractor followed by an early 20hp machine with a string of 20/28's behind it. There is a 'G' series tucked in amongst those and finally four 32/42's. Appropriately, out of shot beyond the carriages is a First World War 40hp armoured Simplex bringing up the rear. Not all could have been under their own power, the G at least would be too slow, but there should have been plenty of power in hand to pull the four carriages making up the train. The upper shot on page 15 is very approximately where this picture was taken long before all the houses were built.                                              *Courtesy Cliff Thomas*

In 1979/80 Motor Rail supplied twelve 60S locomotives to Bord na Móna, the Irish national peat organisation. These were largely used for service trains providing fuel and lubricants to machinery working out on the bogs. Top left is SMH 60SL744 with such a train at Boora in 1982. Of 3ft gauge, these were based on the 60S design at 5 tons weight, but the L in the number denotes that they were fitted with a Lister HA3 air-cooled engine. Although the design was improved with soundproofed cabs, Motor Rail did not carry the process through as well as they might have done, leaving them difficult to maintain. This may have had a bearing on their not obtaining a follow-on order for thirty-five of these locos, although in fairness that order was never placed anywhere. The inset shows a trio of these machines on the multi-gauge track in the works yard at Bedford. In 2018 two of these locomotives, SMH 60SL738 and 751, named respectively *Otter* and *Pig*, were working on a major track re-laying contract on the Manx Electric Railway, on the Isle of Man. *Pig* has no doubt had to stop for the road crossing and is seen pulling away in a suitable cloud of exhaust with a mini excavator and some ballast in tow, the latter possibly to help balance the load. *Top picture courtesy Ian Biscoe; bottom Auldwyn Construction Ltd*

A locomotive rarely seen at all and still less so at work is MR 8970 of 1945 at the Curragh camp of the Irish Army. Following delivery to Baldonnal Airport, Dublin, it had a tour of duty through various military establishments before coming to the Curragh where it was used to transport targets onto the live firing ranges. The locomotive remains on site and ready for use but apparently the track has deteriorated to the point where the whole railway is unusable. As usual the cost of replacement is considerable and its restoration remains in abeyance.

*Courtesy Adrian Nicholls*

Not all peat cutting operations in Ireland were in the hands of Bord na Móna and Midland Irish Peat Co. Ltd had a substantial operation near Mullingar in the Irish Midlands. Here they had a wide variety of locomotives of which this 20/28 was one of the more standard. MR 9543 of 1950 started life at the Isleworth Sewage Works of Middlesex County Council and came to Alan Keef Ltd when the dealers ME Engineering Ltd closed. It has been re-engined with a Deutz F3L912 engine and has had small amount of compensating weight added in Ireland. A sister locomotive was fitted with solid rubber tyres which significantly improved haulage capacity and lasted a surprisingly long time before needing renewal.

A train loaded with jerry cans of petrol to fuel the British Army of the Rhine, at Arsbeck, near Dusseldorf. This was a major petrol distribution point and had a fleet of 20/28 Simplex locomotives in regular use. These no doubt came from the very large number of the type built for the military during the Second World War. With some 50km of track the system covered a large area so that a disaster in one place would not affect the rest of the depot. It is a possibility that the whole facility was set up by the Germans during the war and the British merely took it over. Although this picture dates from 1975, the operation continued until about 1990, by which time spares for the 2DWD engines would have been completely unobtainable.

Here we have Little and Large for comparison. On the rare occasions when they occur, narrow gauge crossings with standard gauge are often very crude affairs but this one is solidly engineered as one would expect from the army. The 0-6-0 main line shunter of around 200hp was built by Andrew Barclay Sons & Co. Ltd in 1966 as one of a batch of four. It was constructed to continental loading gauge and standards to be compatible with DB rolling stock. The comparison with the Simplex is striking.

*Both courtesy Col. David Ronald*

Through the 1950s around eighty locomotives were sold to Sweden through RMP and their local agent Carl Strom. After this Carl Strom became one of the few agents anywhere in the world that were independent of the RMP connection. He even had his own nameplates fitted to locomotives he supplied. Later still, and probably initiated by delays in supply from Bedford, he started manufacturing Simplex spares in Sweden for subsequent sale (much the same thing happened in South Africa). Understandably, when Motor Rail found out about this there was a mighty falling out and that was the end of his agency and sales to Sweden. Above is MR 5761 of 1955, working at the timber treatment plant of Kungle Vattenfallstryrelsen at Asbro in central Sweden in 1971. This is a 12 ton 85hp machine built to 1435mm gauge (effectively standard gauge) and is fitted with air brakes and side buffers for use with mainline wagons and a lower coupling for the treatment plant bogies seen here.

This is a 20/28 MR 9289 of 1948, supplied to the same customer through the same channels and seen on the same date as above. Originally built to 600mm gauge, it has been converted to standard gauge locally and appears to utilise wheels and axleboxes from the timber bogies shown above.

Possibly in this guise it could go right into the pressure tanks in which the wood was treated.

Note 5761 in the background, the very light track (for standard gauge) and the endless pile of sleepers.

*Both courtesy Bjorn Berenstrom*

A classic scene from 1959 in Sweden. MR 9221 of 1946 was sold through Carl Strom to Hoganasbolaget at Nyvang but here it is at Hyllinge Brickworks, near Halsingborg in the south of the country. This 3½ ton loco was built to the unusual gauge of 625mm and, even if relatively young in locomotive terms, the vertical exhaust pipe seems to be the only deviation from original condition. Almost of more interest is the bucket excavator in the background which, like the Butterley pits on pages 25 & 28, appears to be taking a fairly shallow layer of clay from the surface. There were at one time a number of these machines in use by UK brickworks.

MR 9582 of 1951 was supplied by Carl Strom to Stockholm Waterworks, but in 1975 was with Heby Brickworks, some 40km north west of Uppsala. Some intriguing additions seem to have been made to this 3½ locomotive, most notably the shroud from the radiator which one presumes is some form of cab heating. This appears to be most carefully fitted to the bonnet cover but then how does one raise that to start the engine? These engines were not offered with electric start but perhaps this one has been retrofitted. The cab has been raised possibly simply for driver comfort but then what purpose do the rubbing strips along the frame serve? Otherwise the machine is in very smart condition.
*Both courtesy Bo Gyllenberg*

MR 26001 of 1958 has the distinction of being the first of what became the 40S locomotive. As such it was exhibited by or through RMP at the Utrecht Fair of that year. In these locomotives the old faithful Dorman 2DWD engine was replaced by the 2LB of 40hp, the frame shortened and a lever handbrake fitted. Having been sold to Dutch agents Polytex it would appear it did not arrive with Purit NV for use on their peat operation in Klazienaveen, Drenthe, until 1969; its intermediate history is not known. Built to the common Dutch gauge of 700mm it is here seen with a substantial train of empties in 1986 and the photographer described it as the only time he met with it 'in the wild'! Note the large and non-original sandbox on the back of the cab, needed for the climb up from the peat workings to more substantial ground.
*Courtesy Toon Steenmeyer*

A mystery photograph. This was the only railway picture amongst a quantity of photographs bought at a car boot sale. On the back it carries the caption; 'A safe form of transport working for the Germans', from which one presumes that it is taken in Germany although the architecture of the buildings in the background looks remarkably British. The 'building' on the left appears as though it might be a grounded railway vehicle with a lean-to at the end, perhaps covering an open balcony. There is washing hanging on the fence beyond the loco. The locomotive itself is a standard 6 ton 40hp of First World War vintage or immediately afterwards. It certainly still has its Dorman 4JO petrol engine but the curved ends have been removed to reduce weight. The wagons are typical Koppel and are not yet coupled to the locomotive. The driver has perhaps run round his train and may be lighting a cigarette to help him keep warm on what looks like a very cold day in early spring. From dates on other pictures in the collection it could be post Second World War but the 1920s or 1930s seems more likely. The later date might be confirmed by the merest glimpse of a similar looking railway in a recent (2018) television programme about the Berlin airlift and Tempelhof Aerodrome. *Courtesy Tracy Hartley*

In this posed shot are believed to be the first two Simplex Locomotives to be sent to the cane fields of Queensland, Australia. If so, these are 2089 and 2090 of 1922, both 4 ton 20hp tractors and they are crossing the Barron River Bridge near Cairns on the line to Redlynch Station. One of the men here could well be Frank Impey who was sent out from Bedford to commission these two locos, decided to settle in Australia and lived in Cairns for the rest of his life. He is reputed to have lived initially in the packing cases in which the locos were sent out.
*Courtesy John Browning*

# Oceania

This is 6 ton 32/42 MR 10450 of 1955, also on the Redlynch line of Hambledon Mill with a very traditionally loaded train of cut cane in 1964. Simplex locos continued to be used here as their low cab height allowed them to pass under a railway bridge to where the train could be picked up by a main line, but still 2ft gauge, locomotive. Note the exhaust whistle atop the exhaust pipe and the 'string' with which to operate it. The driver is checking his weighbills for the individual consignors of the wagons in his train.
*© Ted Ward, courtesy John Browning*

RIGHT: Having moved off the main line to allow a loaded cane train to pass, ever faithful 20/28 MR 7369 of 1939 is returning to its track repair duties at Seaforth on the Farleigh Mill system, Queensland in 1977. It looks almost as though the crew have brought their bungalow with them but no doubt this is to give shelter from the sun either for work or meal breaks. This locomotive had a very varied life, having originally been bought by Glasgow Corporation Housing Department and delivered to their Robroyston contract. The record notes a spares enquiry from the State Electricity Commission, presumably Australia, in 1960.
© *John Browning*

LEFT: In the early 2000s the locomotive shown above moved to the Cobdogla Museum on the Murray River where, with Alan Keef Ltd's advice, it was re-engined with a Perkins 3.152 engine and fitted with new cab for use on the museum's passenger railway. This is its first commercial outing and note the fire bowser included in the train: standard equipment with their steam locomotive. The Cobdogla Museum's main claim to fame is the Humphrey irrigation pump. This remarkable pump is fired by producer gas and the water forms the piston in what is effectively a four-stroke engine. This delivers about 12 tons of water per stroke or 1,400,000 gallons per hour. It was the second largest installation of its type in world with the largest being at Chingford, England. Both operated into the 1960s.

*Courtesy Dean Adamson*

In later years Simplex locomotives moved to shunting the mill yards and working with maintenance trains whist main haul was transferred to Clyde and Baldwin (of Castle Hill, Australia, not the USA) locomotives in the 200/300hp range, way beyond anything Motor Rail would consider. These, in turn, have been supplanted by the conversion to 2ft gauge of 3ft 6ins and standard gauge double bogie locomotives of 700hp plus, which are often worked in multiple or as distributed power along the train with hauls that can be 60 miles each way. Above we have MR 11255 of 1964 shunting 'bins' for chopped cane into the repair shop at Victoria Mill, near Ingham, Queensland in 1977. The cab has been raised, as have the driver's seat and controls, so that he can see over his train.

This is a 6 ton 32/42 MR 10232 of 1951 in Macknade Mill yard in 1975 with a train of bulk sugar 'boxes'. These are necessarily kept pretty clean, providing the 'as new' look, and are still used to carry sugar to waiting ships at Lucinda Terminal.
*Both © John Browning*

Anything looking less like a Simplex locomotive is hard to imagine but underneath there somewhere is MR 3711 of 1924! The 2JO petrol engine has almost certainly been replaced with a diesel by the time this picture was taken in 1977. Just how the driver gets to his seat and then what he can see of his surroundings is another matter entirely. The place is Caribbean Gardens at Scoresby, in suburban Melbourne, Victoria. It has to be said that the bodywork is a remarkably good representation of the classic American 'F' units of the early dieselisation era.

This one does at least have the Simplex buffer/coupling block but otherwise one could be forgiven for not believing that this is MR 21543 of 1956. The frame seems to have been extended in all directions and whether it retains its original engine and transmission is not obvious. Normally used for maintenance duties it is here hauling a passenger train in 1999 and it is again a smart conversion to a new use at Dreamworld, Coomera, Queensland. Both these locomotives would have been imported for sugar cane haulage but have been overtaken by the ever increasing scale of that industry.

*Both © John Browning*

**RIGHT**: PW28 is a 9 ton locomotive, MR 9040 of 3ft 6ins gauge, supplied to Flower, Davies & Johnson Ltd of Perth in 1953, presumably acting as agents for the Public Works Department of Western Australia. Having been abandoned in the 1960s, it was preserved by local interests and is here seen in commercial use again in 2009 with a maintenance train on Carnarvon Jetty, around 600 miles north of Perth. The jetty was used for the import and export of materials and produce (primarily wool) from this very remote area and the tramway on it was the fourth to be constructed for the purpose. It has been re-engined with a Perkins engine and hydraulic transmission. The white line to the right of the building is the handrail of the 1.6 km jetty stretching out into the Indian Ocean. A tourist train operates on the jetty using a home-built steam outline locomotive.

**BELOW**: Four more of these locomotives were supplied in 1955/7 and PW23 may be one of those. It was used for the same purpose at Point Samson some 400 miles north of Carnarvon, where the jetty was primarily used for the export of asbestos which ceased in 1966. By 1978 the loco had been abandoned in the permanent way yard. The use of these jetties waned as roads were improved in the 1960s and heavy haul rail appeared for the transport of iron ore. This one is in near original condition and is air brake fitted with the compressor and air tank being clearly visible. These places are still remote; a tourist website for Point Samson states that the population was 231 in 2016 and falling. It is hard to believe that at one time this was Western Australia's third largest port.

*Both courtesy Jim Bisdee*

This has to be a classic photograph from 1961. MR 2129 was bought by the North Coast Steam Navigation Co. Ltd in 1923 to operate the short branch to Byron Bay on the outskirts of Sydney, New South Wales. It had various owners over the years and was fitted with a David Brown diesel engine in 1981 by F.J. Walker Ltd, who additionally used it to serve their 'meat works' which closed in 1984. The 'train' is here comprised of an ex-Melbourne cable car; the locomotive still exists, having been restored by its last driver and is now in the care of the local authority.
*Courtesy Noel Reed,*
*per John Browning*

MR 10457 of 1955 was originally supplied per RMP to Russell, Searle Ltd, presumably their local agents, for the State Forestry Commission in New Zealand. Although the Simplex with its cross engine and gearbox is not the most conventional of locomotives, it would have been much more normal than some of the remarkable home-built machines used on New Zealand's logging railways. This is the 32/42hp model fitted with a Dorman 2DL engine and weighed in at 7 tons on 3ft 6ins gauge. By 1980 it had migrated to the Matamara Dairy where it was presumably used to shunt mainline wagons. Note the chopper coupling mounted in the top of the buffer block and the crude shunter's platform below it. The bodywork has been drastically modified, but whether to accommodate a different engine and/or transmission or simply to allow the driver to stand up is not known. Although still in industrial surroundings it does not look as though it has been used for a while.
*Courtesy Ted Lidster*

The old and the new. Above is MR 2046 of 1920 in Lautoka mill yard, Fiji in 1943. This is identical with the 2½ ton locomotives built in such numbers for the First World War although it looks as though it has had some extra weight added on the back corner. It certainly has the original gearbox, radiator and very possibly its Dorman 2JO petrol engine. It was sold to dealers or agents in Sydney and somehow found its way to Fiji. The atmospheric view below, also in Lautoka yard, shows SMH 122U136 with an endless string of cane wagons in 1994. This was one of a pair bought in 1973, followed by two more in 1976. These locos weighed 10 tons and were fitted with Dorman 6DA air-cooled engines of 95hp. It is making up a formation for the Australian-built Clyde diesel of maybe 250hp at right which is waiting for its train before departing. At the time of writing, two out of the four are still at work although they have been re-engined and as a consequence the bonnet line has been raised slightly. Note the cab roof extensions to help keep out sun and tropical storms.
*Courtesy John Maxwell and © John Browning*

Also in Fiji is MR 23014 of 1959, a 10 ton 100hp locomotive of 2ft gauge fitted with a Dorman 5LB engine. This was the largest of the Simplex range at the time and continued with the conventional cross engine and gearbox. It is a beefed up version of the 65hp 9 ton locomotive and Fiji was one of the last places to use this type commercially. Fitted with a flashing warning light, it is seen (*right*) with a train of ash hoppers at Lautoka Mill in 1994. In its new role as motive power for the Coral Creek Railway, a tourist line using a small part of the sugar railway system (*below*), it appears remarkably original although the bonnet line looks slightly higher, perhaps to accommodate its conversion to the hydraulic drive that it now has. It still carries its original fleet number, 8.
© *John Browning and courtesy Justin Cheary*

South Africa was far and away Motor Rail's largest market with approximately 880 locomotives having been supplied, largely to the mining industry. A. Gloster, who was the predecessor of RMP, on one occasion ordered no fewer than 200 locomotives in one batch. Having said that, the company never really got to grips with the boom situation in South Africa and despite having a manufacturing facility in the country eventually lost out to internal competition and, to some extent, the duplicity of their local agents. However, above we have what Motor Rail described as the short frame 20/28. It was still with the Dorman 2DWD engine but had acquired the axleboxes, radiator and lever handbrake that were to be typical of the 40S, and in 3½ ton form is in the workshop yard at the Buffelsfontein Gold Mining Co. Ltd, Stillfontein, in 1984. Below is another in the timber yard at the same mine, but this one has been rebuilt with a new, apparently longitudinal, engine and almost certainly hydraulic drive. Both have acquired an extra ballast weight at the driver's end and these were original fitments and peculiar to South Africa. These may be MR 21091 and 21108 of 1956 and thus would be part of the aforementioned order. Locomotives were rebuilt indiscriminately to suit local requirements and indeed one of the mines built at least seventy new locomotives in their own workshops.                   © *John Middleton*

RIGHT: Trains of sugar cane have been described as a travelling hedge and this one in South Africa amply demonstrates the description. MR 14043 of 1959 is a 9 ton of 48/65hp and of 600mm gauge. It is looking shiny and possibly nearly new at Zululand Sugar Planters.

LOWER RIGHT: With Belville Estates at Mposa is another 9 ton, MR 14020 of 1954, with yet one more hiding in the shed. These two have an earlier and more traditional style of bonnet cover, similar to the 3½ ton 20/28, MR 20540 of 1954, which is passing with a train of empties. *Both Courtesy Frank Jux.*

BELOW: In neighbouring Mozambique this slightly grainy photograph from 1950 shows the first sisal train across the 'new bridge' over the Liunga River, and the locomotive appears to be carrying most of the management staff on this proving run. The previous one had been washed away in floods that raised the river level by at least fifteen feet. It is recorded that 1,350 tons of stone were used in the rebuild. The locomotive is yet another 3½ ton 20/28. The line connected the Namagao Estate, near Nacala, with the Nambilane factory. Note the aerial ropeway in the background, also used for the delivery of sisal leaf to the mill. *Courtesy Wigglesworth & Co. Ltd*

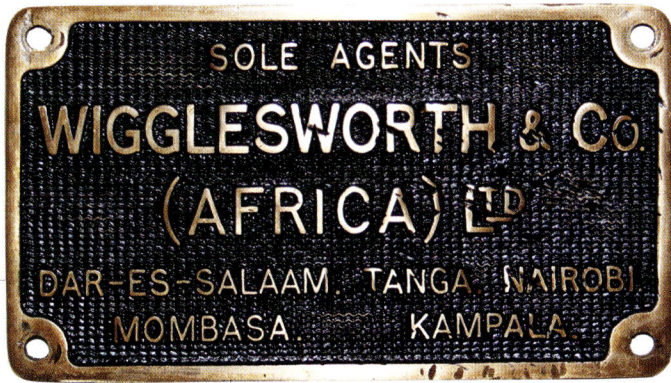

East Africa was Motor Rail's second largest market with some 550 locomotives being supplied primarily to the sisal industry. In practice Wigglesworth were possibly the company's largest single customer as they preferred to buy locomotives themselves and then distribute them to their own and other customer's estates whereas in South Africa locomotives were sold through a variety of organisations including Motor Rail's subsidiary company there. These plates were fitted to the bonnet sidesso that customers knew where to go for spare parts.

**ABOVE**: A 32/42 is crossing a substantial bridge on the Pongwe Estate, near Tanga, on its way to the Pingani Mill in 1948 with a train of cut sisal leaf. The record suggests that some of the earliest of these locomotives sold to Wigglesworth only weighed in at 3 tons, which is surprising to say the least. Without the usual underslung ballast weights they could well have been 4 tons and this looks like one of those, with the overall canopy being a local addition. At this weight they would have been reasonably kind to the lightly laid track but the 5 ton versions, and more particularly the later 5½ ton 60S, would have been another matter. Whilst these would undoubtedly have hauled more sisal it would have been at the expense of the track and may well have had a bearing on the ultimate demise of these once extensive railways.

*Courtesy Wigglesworth & Co. Ltd*

**LEFT**: In the 1990s an attempt was made to revitalise sisal leaf haulage by rail at Lugongo Estate, also near Tanga, and a pair of 3½ ton 20/28's were re-engined with Perkins 3.152 engines. This is one of them on a proving run being watched over by one of the locals and with, shall we say, some interesting trackwork to be seen. A change of management brought back the big engine policy which doomed this useful experiment and the all-conquering tractor and trailer eventually took over.

LEFT: My introduction to the sisal railways of East Africa was at Kiribanga Estate which was part of the Amboni/Wigglesworth group. This was a large estate and the railway included a tunnel under the main Tanga–Korogwe road. The 5 ton 32/42 locomotive is delivering portable track to reach another area where the sisal is ready to cut. Note the cage on the cab roof for tools, etc.

ABOVE: This 32/42 at Amboni Central Workshops may be awaiting a call from one of the many estates in the group to return to work, a call that possible never came. The pulley visible through the revised bonnet covers suggests that it has had a Dorman LB series engine fitted in place of the original 2DL.

ABOVE: In my visits to estates around the country this was more what I was likely to see. An unknown 60S at an unknown estate where the rail system had been abandoned. This one looks as though only minimal work would have been required to have it working again.

RIGHT: This one was reputedly in running order and used occasionally. This establishment was different in that there was a mill on site that made carpets from the sisal produced. This seemed to produce the large amounts of waste seen here that threaten to engulf the loco.

Kikwetu Estate, near Lindi, and not far from the Mozambique border, with a 3½ ton 20/28 that is very possibly one of a batch of seven of these locomotives supplied in 1946/47, all rebuilt from those supplied to The War Office. At the end of the Second World War many of the by then surplus locomotives were offered back to the original manufacturers for them to sell elsewhere, no doubt at a useful profit/discount for all concerned. The overall roof is very smart and may have been supplied with the loco, although the record does not state such.
*Courtesy Wigglesworth & Co. Ltd*

Kikwetu was a large estate and it is worth recording that the last locomotive to be wholly built at Bedford was supplied here in 1986. As its number suggests, 60SP756 was fitted with a Perkins 4.236 engine, a type that proved not to be successful in these locomotives due to vibration problems. As a consequence, when I saw it some three years later it was derelict. I put a good deal of effort into proposals for the rehabilitation of the railways on this estate, which was by then no longer part of the Wigglesworth 'empire', but nothing came of it largely due to lack of money.

This is a delightful picture of the workforce on its way to the cane fields of Sena Sugar at Luabo, Mozambique, in 1974. The locomotive is the usual 3½ ton 20/28 and the track is good so the train is probably making good speed. The bonnets were always convenient places for the second – or third – man to sit but the practice did nothing for their longevity. Note how the fender bar has been raised and the coupling chain positioned below it, no doubt to suit the wagons in use. Regrettably this large and extensive system was a casualty of the independence wars of the area. *Courtesy Geoff Cooke*

Also on their way to work but this time in Cameroon and in perhaps rather safer conditions! The locomotive is one of a batch of nine 'U' series locomotives classified as 117U and 118U supplied through RMP in 1968. This is one of the smaller 5 ton 117U's fitted with Deutz F4L912 engines of 47hp. The larger model would have looked the same but had ballast weights to bring it up to 8 tons and been fitted with the six-cylinder version of the same engine. This is circa 1970 at Tiko, where the railway served the extensive rubber and banana plantations of the Cameroon Development Corporation. *Courtesy Frank Jux*

Ghana. These three locomotives of 3ft 6ins gauge were supplied through RMP, the first two to British Aluminium Co. Ltd and the third to Ghana Bauxite Ltd who were no doubt a local interest partnership. Bauxite is the ore from which aluminium is smelted. 5 ton 32/42, MR 10398 of 1953, looks a little woebegone but appears to be complete; the wear on the buffer head suggest that it must see some use – or at worst it's simply a buffer stop.

In 1982, when both Ghanian pictures were taken, 7 ton MR 60S400 of 1971 appears to be well thought of, judging by the smiling faces of local staff at Takoradi. The buffer arrangement is likely to be a local addition although the driver's canopy would be original. I used this picture in a Simplex leaflet soon after the takeover and somebody, somewhere, but not in Ghana, said to me, 'I know that man in the white shirt!' It's a small world out there.

To complete the scene is an ex-works picture of 60SD757 of 1987. This was built in association with Alan Keef Ltd very shortly before production ceased at Bedford. Therefore it carries an MR not an AK works number. It is seen here soon after Alan Keef Ltd moved to Herefordshire and awaits the fitting of its ballast weights and buffers. Being a 60SD, and therefore fitted with a Deutz air-cooled engine, it would been only 6 tons weight and had standard buffers which may well have been altered upon arrival in Ghana.

Another 4 ton 32/42, also in 1948 but this time south of Tanga at the Kigombe Estate. The train is carrying bales of sisal fibre to the godown, or warehouse. Once the sisal fibre is separated from the leaf it is dried on racks in the sun (usually transferred by a hand worked railway), then baled and stored before transfer to the nearest port, in this case Tanga, for overseas shipment. It was a feature of locomotives in the sisal fields that they were often hung around with lengths of (sisal) rope, presumably for hauling wagons on an adjoining track. The length of pipe slung along the side is no doubt for assisting with the righting of de-railed wagons. What appear to be ballast weights here are in fact baulks of timber to act as crash bars if the locomotive itself should de-rail. A slightly better canopy has been added to this locomotive.

*Courtesy Wigglesworth & Co. Ltd*

This is almost certainly the same locomotive, and driver, on the same occasion, but this time out in the fields with a train of sisal leaf for transport to the mill. It also looks as though there is at least one wagon behind the locomotive which will have to be collected as well. Note the rogue sisal growing in the boscage beside the track. In the fields themselves, sisal was, and is, planted in ruler-straight lines at a precise spacing giving an overall chequerboard effect.

*Courtesy Wigglesworth & Co. Ltd*

Around sixty-five locomotives were supplied to Ghana between 1956 and 1971, mostly for work in the Ashanti goldfields. This included the first fifteen of the 'G' series, which order must have assisted in the company achieving a Queen's Award to Industry for Export Achievement in 1969. Here we have a late series 20/28 leaving the East Adit at the Obuasi Mine with a train of Granby cars loaded with ore for crushing. This mine was both shaft and adit worked. The loco is still fitted with the Dorman 2DWD engine and old-style bonnet covers, but the radiator is now the flat topped variety and, under enlargement, it can be seen to have the wheelsets and axleboxes that would become standard with the 40S. The engine is still hand start but was fitted with a dynamo to charge the battery for lighting. The large black box beside the radiator is the exhaust conditioner for underground use. The Granby cars have side doors which open automatically when the wagon is tipped. It can only be guesswork but the loco could be one of those supplied in the late 1950s. Both locomotive and wagons look reasonably new which may be why this official photograph was taken.   *Courtesy John Middleton*

At the Ndola copper mines of ZCCM in Zambia are MR 119UA087 of 1970 and an unidentified 9 ton locomotive. The latter may well be one of a batch of fourteen supplied in 1954/5 although there were a few supplied later. Note the 'skirts' on the 'U' series to cover the wheels at the wider than usual gauge of 3ft 6ins, and also the dual couplings on the 9 ton allowing it to shunt both internal and mainline rolling stock (the 'standard' gauge for southern Africa is 3ft 6ins). This picture is probably posed and taken by John Palmer, who was a design engineer with Motor Rail, when on a visit to the Zambia mines in 1971. He continued in the same capacity with Alan Keef Ltd until he retired.

SIMPLEX LOCOMOTIVES AT WORK

LEFT: Those involved in the traffic incident in the foreground are oblivious to the lonely locomotive crossing a village centre in Somalia. This is either SMH 117U140 or 141, of 1974 supplied through RMP to Societa Nazionale Agricola Industriale (SNAI) to haul sugar cane to Jawhor mill. There were also 60S locomotives here along with a number of from Deutz and Schoma. The whole project collapsed in internal conflict within the country and although there are proposals to start growing sugar again it is unlikely that rail haulage will be used. *Courtesy Alan Bird*

BELOW: One can deduce from the position of the driver that he is pushing an empty train out into the cane fields for another load. Unusually, here the train is comprised of bogie wagons with the cane loaded longitudinally upon them, hence the protective grille on the rear window to give the driver some protection in the event of a sudden stop or derailment.

The first 'T' series locomotives built by Motor Rail went to Tanganyika Planting Co. Ltd (TPC) at Moshi in Tanzania, with the fleet eventually reaching eleven locomotives together with four 'U' series. This may be 100T010 of 1975 backing a train of sugar cane across the main access road to the mill in 1989. All weighed 12 tons and were fitted with Dorman 6DA air-cooled engines rated at 95hp with hydrostatic transmissions. The boy on the bonnet, and apparently clinging onto the exhaust pipe, is there to tell the driver if the train should start to de-rail. As these locomotives were intended for mining work, which they never did, Motor Rail did not produce a surface version similar to the conversions later done by Alan Keef Ltd (see pages 35 & 37). Note the crossing keepers hut made up from metre gauge and 2ft gauge steel sleepers and intended to keep out the sun rather than rain.

On the other side of the mill and under wide open African skies, another member of the fleet is propelling a train through complicated trackwork towards the weighbridge for subsequent unloading. To give an idea of the scale of operations here, there is in the order of 50 miles of track and the mill and offices are 12 miles from the main gate. Four of these locomotives were re-engined with Perkins engines, JCB transmissions and shaft drive to the wheels by Alan Keef Ltd, and these are still at work although the longer distance haulage has been taken over by a small number of larger and more powerful locomotives built by Schöma of Germany.

SIMPLEX LOCOMOTIVES AT WORK

# Asia & the Middle East

**TOP**: East India Tramways came before Motor Rail existed, or even thought about building locomotives, and it was for this organisation that John Dixon Abbott developed his equal-speed forward and reverse gearbox which became the hallmark of the Simplex locomotive. The company continued to operate the tramways in Karachi up to the partition of India in 1949 when the concern was sold to Mohamedali Tramways who continued to operate it until 1975. Here we have two very smart cars (they did not work in multiple), perhaps at Boulton Market which was the hub of the system and possibly towards the end of Motor Rail's tenure. Motor Rail must have lost out heavily with the sale of EIT as they supplied most of the company's requirements – from brake blocks, 300 at a time, ticket card by the ton and even a steam roller.

**MIDDLE**: The advertising boards and the Mohamedali Tramways roundel on the strengthened dash indicate that this picture dates to after the takeover by local interests. The conductor can be seen taking fares whilst standing on the longitudinal footboard. The car is headed for Cantonment station apparently on one of the leafier routes.

**BOTTOM**: This picture just had to be included! Is the Renault Dauphine beating the tram or vice versa? With Karachi obviously becoming a modern city the trams may have been seen as anachronistic, but reputedly it was the activities of the local transport mafia that actually caused their closure. Certainly Mohamedali Tramways were talking to Motor Rail about new cars in the late 1960s.

**ABOVE:** East India Tramways again. Two cars pull into the kerb loading point at Boulton Market in the later years of the system. The destination of leading car No. 151 is Gandhi Gardens. Note the sand deposited beside the rails and used to help the cars start with a heavy load.
*Per Andrew Neale*

On trial before being sent off to work. This is one of a pair of 40SD locomotives, MR 40SD505 and 506 of 1977, which together with a three-coach train and track were supplied by Alan Keef Ltd to the Imperial Iranian Navy in the days of the Shah. The two locomotives were actually RMP stock locos of which they were divesting themselves at that time, which aided a delivery period of only twelve weeks. The navy had a ship moored at the end of a lengthy jetty in their naval base at Bandar Abbas and this was to be used as barracks for naval personnel. The train was their means of transport back to the shore. In the inset can be seen the electrical and air brake connections for both loco and train, the latter being something Motor Rail said could not be done. The train was fitted with cushioned seats and electric lighting, but only a fancy canvas roof. Remarkably, a locomotive with an Alan Keef Ltd plate on it was seen in Damascus many years later and could only have been one of these two, but regrettably no photograph was taken of it.

This typifies the problem with finding pictures of Simplex locomotives in India, as was mentioned in the introduction. The photographer no doubt went to the Kandri Mine of Manganese Ore India Ltd in Maharashtra State in 1971 to photograph the Jung steam locomotive; the fact that there is a Simplex locomotive as well is sheer chance – unless, of course, it was used to pull the other from its shed. Both locos are in spotless condition and the 2½ ton 20/28 is fitted with an alternative bonnet style required by Parry & Co., RMP's agents in India, doubtless to improve the appearance (see comment page 48). This is thought to be one of two supplied through RMP in 1953 or 1954 but the record is blank as to final destination throughout those years.

This is almost certainly the other of the pair supplied at that time. This may be a case of the photographer feeling duty bound to take a picture of the diesel loco and its proud crew when it is actually the steam loco that he wants to photograph! Note the man 'hand tramming' at least one wagon load of material at left.

*Both courtesy Simon Darvil*

Despite being nearly thirty years old when this picture was taken in 1989 at the Samastipur Sugar Factory, near Patna, MR 22088 of 1960 looks to be in almost as-new condition and certainly the green paint is 'very Simplex'. This is a 4½ ton metre gauge machine, fitted with a Dorman 2LB engine of 40hp and has outside wheels because of the gauge. According to the build sheets the overall canopy together with the chopper coupling and its housing were 'add-on' extras to the standard build. Sugar cane has obviously arrived in four-wheel vans on the local railway and is being unloaded into the conveyor on the right. *Courtesy Lawrence Marshal, per Andrew Neale*

BELOW: This is either MR 2258 or 2259 of 1923 vintage, seen at the factory of Belapur Sugar & Allied Industries Ltd, Harigaon in Maharashtra State in 1971. With the 'bent' frame, buffer/couplers and driving position over the engine, its First World War parentage is very obvious. The original Dorman 4JO petrol engine has been replaced by a Perkins P6 but much else remains the same. As built, the loco weighed 6 tons which would have compared with the ex-WD locos that this factory was reputed to have. Maybe the other locomotives of which we have a glimpse are they, but with the curved ballast weights removed.
*Courtesy Simon Darvill*

MR 14060 of 1963 is a 9 ton 48/63hp locomotive, here seen shunting the exchange sidings with the North Eastern Railway at Hindustan Sugar Mills in 1994. The cab has been raised so that the driver can see over the main line wagons and the tropical roof extended. Note the circulating pump on the radiator fitted for tropical climates. The inscription on the bonnet side states that it has a Dorman engine, a 3DL, and is possibly for the benefit of repair shop fitters. There is a little bit of mystery about this loco: all the published records give it as 2ft gauge but the original build sheets are clear that it is metre gauge and the couplers and so on were part of the build. It cost £2,218 8s 8d but how that compared to the sale price is not recorded. To add to the plot, RMP records give a delivery date of 1958, to the correct customer, but still of 2ft gauge. The unusual frame cut outs would be a local modification done to give better access to the chain tension gear. © *Chris West*

Alexandra Jute Mills had been closed for a while in 1994/5 due to labour troubles when this picture was taken and it is not known whether this 32/42, MR 10111 of 1949, ever worked again – when and if they re-opened. The track looks extremely light but as this loco only weighs four tons they obviously got away with it. The overall canopy would be 'home made'. Unusually the machine was supplied through agents in Dundee, which is perhaps hardly surprising as that city was the centre of the British jute trade. © *Chris West*

Motor Rail sold around thirty locomotives through RMP to the nationalised salt industry in Sri Lanka, then Ceylon. These started off in the 1940s with 20/28's, culminating with a batch of fifteen 40S locos in 1966. This is not Sri Lanka, it is Bowen on the Queensland coast of Australia but the operation and surroundings are likely to be very similar. Sea water will be pumped into the ponds seen here, evaporated by the sun and then scraped into a pile which will be loaded away by train. Note the plates on the wagon ends to stop too much salt dropping between the wagons as the train is drawn past the conveyor. The year is 1983 and the locomotive is MR 8653, one of the many bought by the War Office in 1941. It would appear to have passed through the hands of the dealer, George Bungey in 1951, presumably on its way to Australia. I was once taken to a salt works in Turkey, very similar to this, where I was told there were 'perhaps one or two locos'. I lost count at twenty-seven, but sadly no Simplexes! That operation had a pile of salt maybe 25ft high and a mile and half long with 360° excavators to load it into trains. The second picture is Sri Lanka, but after the industry was privatised in 1996 and tractors and trailers had taken over. This would be one of the 1966 batch of 4½ ton 40S locos set up presumably for visitors to see; it doesn't look as though it has worked for a while.                © *John Browning & Lanka Salt*

In 1972 RMP supplied a complete railway system to Tagerghat Limestone quarry in Bangladesh including seven 7 ton 60S locomotives, works numbers 60S405 – 411. This is one of them in 1995 with a lengthy train of skips and below another that has been re-engined locally with a Deutz F4L912 engine taken from a derelict Schoma locomotive. The young driver is not worried

about such niceties as silencers and air cleaners, or the state of the bodywork, provided his locomotive will pull the train. The lime stone rock as seen above was taken by barge to Chhatak Cement works for conversion into cement and at that time the only access to the site was by water. Whilst this contract was in hand, what was East Pakistan became Bangladesh with considerable warfare and disturbance in the process. It must have been an anxious time for all involved. The quarry itself dates from colonial days with part of the system remaining within India necessitating a customs post on the quarry railway! The operation has now closed, presumably the equipment scrapped and the flooded quarry has become a tourist attraction for the burgeoning Bangladeshi middle class.

A proud driver and his locomotive. This is one of a series of Motor Rail photographs from circa 1971 of palm oil railways in Malaysia, but frustratingly there is no record of just what locomotive or which estate they were taken at. Around this time RMP sold a considerable number of 2½ ton locomotives through various local agents to this industry. This would appear to an early 40S as it has the rounded bonnets, new style radiator and the air cleaner for the Dorman 2LA or 2LB engine, but not the later rounded cab roof. With the shortened frame the sandboxes became prominent and vulnerable in this weight of loco but were contained within the ballast weights in heavier machines. The timbers on the double-skinned tropical cab roof may be there to assist with re-railing wagons if required.

MR7991 of 1947, a 32/42 of 6 tons weight, pushes a well loaded train to the unloading point at Lablis Oil Palm Estate, Johore, Malaysia in 1971. The canopy may or may not be an original fitment. One of the problems with palm oil railways is that the track tends to be covered in oil and so often locomotives were supplied of low horse power but high weight, such as a 5½ ton 40S, to overcome this problem. Light railways are still used extensively in the older estates and at least one such claims to have no less than 500km of track. Most, such as the one above, are 2ft gauge but there some at 700mm in what were Dutch colonies.
*Courtesy J. Benson,*
*per Rob Dickinson*

**ABOVE:** This locomotives is anything but working but I felt it was crying out to be included. It is part of a batch of three, SMH 102T004/5/6 supplied through RMP in 1973 to Pamitran and despatched to Surabaya, Indonesia. They were of 700mm gauge, 12 tons weight and fitted with Deutz F6L912 engines of 96hp. Here it is at Krebet Baru sugar mill near Melang in East Java the early 2000s. The loco has been converted into a crane locomotive, presumably for re-railing cane wagons. The cab has had a substantial fulcrum point built around it with a resting point for the boom over the front buffer. There also seems to be some other sort of hydraulic device mounted on the roof; the whole assemblage probably having been 'designed' around a spare hydraulic ram that they happened to have. Obviously there were no problems with overhead structures on this line! These and other locomotives here have the extended buffing point, because cane is transported longitudinally on the wagons but it could cause derailment issues and hence the reason for *Modiksu*. In this guise the machine has been seriously overloaded as the front springs are visibly broken and part missing.                                    *Courtesy Yoga bagus Prayogo*

**LEFT:** I have deliberately avoided works photographs, not least because Motor Rail were not good at recording what the picture was all about. However, this is SMH 101T017 of 1979, 9 tons and unusually fitted with a Perkins 6.354 engine of 94hp together with hydrokinetic transmission. It was supplied through RMP and Patterson Simons to PNP VII in Indonesia. The significance of the picture is that this is the only occasion when Motor Rail produced what might be termed a surface version of the 'T' series, in this case with bonnets akin to the later 60S's, a vertical sided cab and 60S 7 ton ballast weights. Note also the multi-gauge track extending into the works.

Logging in what was formerly North Borneo but is now Sabah, a state in Malaysia. The rowing boat in the foreground and the small boy on the right say it all! This 32/42 and its train may have been parked here at Segaliud overnight and become surrounded by flood water in January 1951. This is probably one of four locomotives supplied in 1949/50, two of which were, very unusually, supplied as chassis only with the customer fitting the engine and gearbox, maybe from an earlier machine.

This is another departure from Motor Rail's standardised production line. MR 5078 of 1956 is of a type normally supplied in standard gauge (see page 22), but is here of 3ft gauge and weighing in at 12 tons. It is fitted with a Dorman 4DL engine of 85hp and is looking to be in fairly new condition. The train is being loaded with a Thew-Lorrain crawler crane and appears to be very much at the 'end of steel'. Enlarged, the 'tide 'mark' on the frame suggests that somewhere it might have been driven over the end of the track into deep mud!

3ft gauge 10 ton MR 9027 of 1952, with a train of logs in tow, is at Lungmanis. This locomotive was fitted with a Dorman 3DL engine of 48/63hp. Remarkably, these logs may have been moved by hand on greased poles from where they were felled for up to a mile to a railhead where they were again hand loaded onto log bogies. Most logging lines in Borneo were 2ft gauge but this one is a relic of a much earlier operation that included a Shay steam locomotive.
*All courtesy D.M. Robinson collection, per Ross Ibbotson*

Between 1966 and 1970 some thirty-six 5½ ton 60S locomotives were supplied to Sabah through RMP and local agents North Borneo Trading. If one was to make the outrageous suggestion that this was the twelfth of the batch, it would be 60S334, shipped to Sandakan in 1966, which would tie in nicely with this new looking locomotive at Kretam, pictured in 1968. This train, with its attendant staff transport, manager's trolley and empty log bogies, has been shunted into the siding to allow a lengthy train of logs to pass.
*Courtesy Mrs Judith Robertson, per Ross Ibbotson*

Described as 'swamp logging', this was timber extraction in the coastal plain or on the flat lands close to rivers so that logs could be rafted to the sawmills or direct for export. The scene here is part of the operation by Chung Chao Lung (West Coast) Ltd and is believed to be at Lumat circa 1963. This company bought a number of 3½ ton 40S locomotives both before and after that date so this is no doubt one of them. The train of logs disappears into the distance so either gradients are minimal or it's all downhill. The timber in the foreground is ramin and behind that jongkong.
*Courtesy Sabah Information Dept, per Ross Ibbotson*

We have a number of pictures with people precariously balanced on locomotives travelling to or from their work. This one is a 20/28 belonging to Yeng Ho Hong Co Ltd on that company's operation at Lamag.
The man in the white shirt is the logging camp manager who had worked for Yeng Ho Hong for more than thirty years. This company bought considerable numbers of new 60S locos but there is no record of 20/28's, so this 3½ ton version must have been acquired second hand. Note the crowbar in use as a coupling pin – or just stored there.
*Courtesy Nicolas Tan collection, per Ross Ibbotson*

Balcarce, Argentina. To use a modern idiom, this is Nocton (see page 18) on steroids, and then some! In 1920 the Buenos Aires Great Southern Railway, better known as Ferrocarril del Sud, built a series of 600mm gauge agricultural lines to feed produce onto its main line for onward transport to Buenos Aires. Balcarce was the largest of the four, there being around 145km of trackage serving some 70,000 hectares of land, with potatoes and grain being the principal crops. These lines were operated by a fleet of largely ex-First World War locomotives that included Hunslet 4-6-0 steam (twenty-six), Simplex 20hp (twenty) and 40hp (thirteen), with a few O&K steam and Baldwin tractors thrown in for good measure. The 20hp tractor above looks a bit lost amongst the sheer number of wagons to be seen. The bogie wagons are some of the 600 supplied by Hudson, the four-wheelers to the right (and in the upper picture below) are just a few of the no fewer than 1,800 in use. The vans previously saw service as ambulance vehicles. Main line track was substantial, although a 'Jubilee' turnout has been inserted at bottom right. These pictures are likely to have been posed and official, not least as, when enlarged, the gentleman in the centre above is wearing a top hat. The Balcarce system also

ran an official passenger service with five typical American-style passenger cars at its disposal. However, the train shown bottom left is very much a 'workmen's' train, with the accommodation made up on Hudson wagons. All the 20hp locos shown have had additional weights added over the wheels, no doubt to increase their haulage ability. Inevitably road transport took over in short order but the lines remained in use into the 1940s, with a few remnants operating up to 1960.
*Courtesy John Dickson and Ferroclub Argentina*

**The Americas**

Although a very poor photograph, there appears to be an ever faithful 20/28 with a train of empty skips at the gypsum quarry of Julio Carrol near the town of Neuquen, Rio Negro Province, Argentina. This operation started in 1935 and closed about 1970. The line was some 15km long and this viaduct is thought to be within the quarry complex. Reputedly the loco hauled empties to the quarry and the train returned by gravity with the loco acting as a brake van. The cab looks as though it may be original but alterations to the rest of the bodywork must have been done locally.
*Courtesy Martin Coombs*

My comments in the introduction about being unable to contact photographers apply to these two pictures. They are both on banana plantations in the Sao Paula area of Brazil. Both are typical 20/28's of the immediate post-war period and indeed something over twenty of this type were sent to Brazil through various local agents. The one centre right has lost its radiator so has presumably been re-engined with an air-cooled engine. This is at Fazenda Aurea in 1994 and bananas appear to be being transferred to rail from a tractor and trailer. Lower right is 1991 on the Fazenda Jatobatuba and the single-wagon train is on its way to the farm centre where the bananas will be graded and packed. The slightly odd position of the wagon is accounted for by the track climbing sharply onto the precarious looking bridge, but none of those with the train look in the least perturbed. From other photos of these lines, a feature seems to be that the track is often completely hidden in high grass.
*Courtesy Coaraci Camargoein and Nilson Rodreigues, per Cid Jose Beraldo*

Modernisation has come to the gypsum quarry opposite in the form of a short frame 40S fitted with the Dorman 2LB engine. The battery and its cover are prominent on the footplate and the lever handbrake can just be seen. The cab roof has been raised, as it often was, to give better access and in this case extra ventilation. The train is well loaded with rock gypsum and the smart little manrider behind the loco suggests that this may be either the last train of the day or there are visitors present.
*Courtesy Martin Coombs*

Another posed photograph. Taken from a Motor Rail & Tramcar Co. Ltd catalogue of 1923, this is simply described as a '40 B.H.P. 6 Ton Type Petrol Locomotive at work in Nitrate Pampas of Chile'. This might be termed the civilian version of the First World War 40hp tractor. If the caption is correct this may be MR 1957 of 1920, which was shipped to Caleta Buena, the terminus of the Agua Santa Railway, where three balanced inclines brought nitrate down the 2,400ft escarpment to the port. Three similar locomotives were shipped to Chile, one each over the next three years, being MR No's 2120, 2130 and 2257. These were all 8 ton versions of the same type, they were shipped through Iquique and may have gone here or to the Junin Railway which was the other major 2ft 6ins railway in the area.
*MR&TC catalogue,
courtesy Jon Bryant*

Following the success of their 8 ton 40hp standard gauge shunter, Motor Rail quite reasonably thought there would be a market for something larger and developed this 65hp 16 ton machine. In 1923 they had the confidence to build three 'on spec' and the fact that they did not all sell for some years may have dampened their thinking on larger locomotives. This is MR 2293 and was not sold until 1926, when it went to the Nitrate Railways of Chile for shunting wagons in Puerto Iquique docks. These locos were dual control, driven from the left-hand side in either direction and used the control system developed for East India Tramways. Although looking reasonably smart, it is actually standing in the scrap siding at the docks and seems to have already lost some components such as buffers.
*Courtesy the late Wilf Simms, per Donald Binns*

There are still Simplex locomotives at work in Chile. This is MR 40S434 of 1973 at Tongo Mine in 2017. It was sold through RMP to Head Wrightson for ENAMI, which was a state organisation that acted as a centralised buying agency for the smaller mines of Chile. Despite being nearly 45 years old it seems to be in remarkably good condition including something close to its original paintwork. As with other pictures herein, where underground working is concerned the exhaust conditioner box is prominent even if painted yellow rather than the more conventional black. The tipping dock looks a bit precarious and one wonders whether it is sheer chance, or not, that there that there seems to be a bit of extra support where the locomotive is standing. *Courtesy Harold Middleton collection*

It is not uncommon for locomotives and/or wagons to be plinthed (see Lanka Salt, page 85), or to use the vernacular, stuffed and mounted, once their *raison d'être* has ceased to exist. This is MR 22203 of 1966 at Cerrillos de Tamaya, near Ovalle, Chile, where it is in the main square. This locomotive had a bad start having been ordered by RMP in 1964, who then cancelled the order. So Motor Rail made it anyway for stock and it was finally sold in 1966. This gives a very good view of the controls with the lever handbrake prominent, two gear change levers poking through the panel, the short one being forward and reverse with the longer first and second gear. The clutch pedal is in front of them, with the throttle being the short lever in the centre. The panel cut-out is for access to the engine

fuel pump with the instrument panel above it. It is sobering to think that by this time the arrangement had existed for fifty years and was to continue for at least another twenty-five. *Courtesy Diego Bugueño Salvo, per Harold Middleton collection*

MR 9933 of 1974 was the last standard gauge shunter to be built by the company and was supplied to Booker Sugar Ltd in Guyana. In this slightly cluttered picture it is waiting to cross the lift bridge to enter the mill for another load of sugar in the containers on its train. These are taken a mile or so to a wharf where they are lifted off and emptied into storage bins to await the arrival of a ship. The climate is hot and humid, as a result of which this loco normally runs with the bonnet covers raised. The lift bridge crosses a canal which is the means of supplying the mill with raw sugar cane. Known locally as punts, these are lifted bodily by the gantry in the background and tipped for emptying. This is very reminiscent of the compartment boats used in the north of England for the transport of coal.

*Courtesy Thomas Kautzor*

3½ ton MR 9411 of 1949 was originally built for the London contractors Holloway Bros but dressed in new clothes was suppled as a service and maintenance locomotive by Alan Keef Ltd to a new railway at the Iguazu Falls in Argentina. It was fitted with a new Perkins 3.152 engine and air brakes so that it could be used for passenger trains if necessary. That was obviously the case in 2015 when it is being thrashed unmercifully to start a heavily loaded train away from the Central Station. Two new AK locomotives and eight carriages were also supplied to this project. It is quite remarkable how many people say they have travelled on an AKL train and it turns out to be this one, but then this operation does carry no less than 1.5 million passengers per annum. Forget the idea that small leisure railways are somehow not a real railway!

From 1965 to 1970, Motor Rail sold over sixty 'U' series locomotives through the local firm of Jarvis Clarke & Co. Ltd to the International Nickel Company of Canada (INCO) for mining operations in the province of Ontario. Photographs of locos working underground are rare and this is possibly the only one of these locos. Note how the locomotive and wagons fit the tunnel like the proverbial glove. They were supplied in both 2ft and 3ft gauge, usually of 7 or 8 tons weight but unusually fitted with either Dorman or Deutz engines of only 45/50hp. It was primarily these locomotives that precipitated the Queens Award to Industry for Export Achievement in 1969. Unfortunately, the Achilles heel of these was the use of Ruston hydraulic motors which gave endless trouble and eventually led to a cessation of this business. Because of this, at one point Motor Rail were out of pocket to the tune of £52,500 (£750,000 today) and Ruston & Hornsby could not have cared less.

Apart from INCO above, effectively no Simplex locomotives went to North America in Motor Rail's time. However, in 2004 Ken Zadnicheck bought MR 22192 of 1962 and named it *Gerrard* for the 2ft gauge railway he was building as part of a new trailer park and entertainment complex at Silverhill, Alabama. The loco was used for the construction of the line (*above*) and at right is seen with a party train in 2018. It was joined by an 0-4-2 steam locomotive from Exmoor Steam Railway to create the Wales West Railway. MR 22129 was one of a pair built for the Trent River Board, with the delivery address being no more than a site described as on the A631 road, ¼ mile east of Bawtry with two DLH hire locos to be collected. It subsequently went to the Alford Valley Railway, near Aberdeen and was there replaced by a new steam outline locomotive from Alan Keef Ltd. Note the 7¼ins gauge track in the foreground of both pictures.                    *Courtesy Ken Zadnichek*